The Boarding School Survival Guide

Praise for *The Boarding School Survival Guide*

"What a great way to introduce oneself to the world of boarding schools! Learn from the experiences of two wonderful Andover students, Justin Muchnick and Bennett Sherr, and their counterparts at other leading schools. This book belongs on the nightstand of any prospective boarding school student and her or his parent."

~ John Palfrey, Head of School, Phillips Academy Andover

"In *The Boarding School Survival Guide,* Justin Muchnick has assembled contributions from more than 20 boarding school students. They're smart, diverse, witty, and helpful—just like the students I meet on my travels to boarding school campuses. The chapters cover a wide range of considerations: from the school search, application, and selection process to life in the classroom, the dining hall, and the dorm. Whether the topic is writing papers or doing your own laundry, the student authors take time to explain and reassure, caution and encourage. Throughout, they speak with genuineness—and with genuine enthusiasm for a little-understood but amazing learning opportunity. If you're planning to attend boarding school, considering it, or simply curious, read this book."

~ Peter Upham, Executive Director, The Association of
Boarding Schools (TABS), BoardingSchools.com

"No one in the boarding school admission office chooses a photo highlighting a student frowning on a rainy, cloudy day as the cover shot for their viewbook. Quite the contrary—bright fall colors, robust smiles, and everyone engaged is the photo sought and selected. Young Mr. Justin Muchnick has cut through the veneer so any student, parent, prospective employee, ANYONE considering life at a boarding school would be well served to peruse this manual and embrace its heartfelt message. What makes it most compelling to me, a 20-plus-year veteran of the boarding school admission arena, is the fact that Muchnick doesn't rely solely on his alma mater, as distinguished as it may be. He has drawn from a cast of contributors representing myriad institutions: public, private, big, small, country, city, etc. Quite simply, he practices what he preaches, and, therefore, *The Boarding School Survival Guide* is now a must read to all my prospective students because it does rain, clouds do materialize, and, yes, frowns are seen on occasion around campus (especially around finals week during Leftover Sunday Dinner!)."

~ Alan D. Whittemore, Dean of Admission,
Maine School of Science & Mathematics

"Attending boarding school is a big decision, and it is an exciting time. The transition period to a boarding school is a different experience for each student and parent. Careful planning can make the transition smoother. Justin's book is a very comprehensive overview of the myriad aspects of boarding school that people simply do not think about. *The Boarding School Survival Guide* covers it all—A to Z. It is a must read for any family preparing for boarding school."

~ Joe Hemmings, Assistant Head of School for
Enrollment, Hebron Academy

"Muchnick set out to find other students from different boarding schools who could write a chapter on their own experiences. . . . [He] found inspiration from his own personal boarding school application process. Each chapter explains a different characteristic of boarding school by using examples of the writer's personal experiences and also offers broad advice about the topic. From academics, to athletics, to dorm life, the book explores all the features of boarding school."

~ The Phillipian

"Any decent boarding school creates its own subculture. It has its own set of conventions, traditions, rules, expectations, and celebrations. Stepping into this world is a bit like culture shock, and can overwhelm a new student. By studying these vignettes of boarding school life, any prospective student will get a sense for what's to come. They can make an informed decision about whether this world is right for them, and how best to adjust once they enter it. Boarding school is an all-consuming, immensely rewarding experience. This book will prepare you to enter that world."

~ Brett Potash, Dean of Students, The Webb Schools

The Boarding School Survival Guide

Justin Ross Muchnick

 PETERSON'S

About Peterson's

Peterson's provides the accurate, dependable, high-quality education content and guidance you need to succeed. No matter where you are on your academic or professional path, you can rely on Peterson's print and digital publications for the most up-to-date education exploration data, expert test-prep tools, and top-notch career success resources—everything you need to achieve your goals.

For more information, contact Peterson's, 3 Columbia Circle, Suite 205, Albany, NY 12203; 800-338-3282 Ext. 54229; or find us online at www.petersonsbooks.com.

For my loving family

Acknowledgments

I could not have written this book without the help and support of many people. Thank you to Bernadette Webster and Robyn Thurman at Peterson's for believing in, supporting, and allowing me the experience and platform to create and produce this project. Julie Ammermuller, Stephanie Benyo, and Jill Schwartz at Peterson's also helped edit and promote this book. I am grateful to my mom for assisting with many of the behind-the-scenes details so that I could focus on the writing and editing of the book. We shared many laughs and conversations relating to this project. To my dad, siblings, grandparents, and Ziggy, I love you all. And, finally, I am grateful to my co-authors and the hundreds of students from near and far who took the time to submit chapters and share their stories. I have more than enough content for a sequel!

~ *Justin Ross Muchnick*

Contents

CONTENTS

CONTENTS

CONTENTS

INTRODUCTION:
Why I Wrote *The Boarding School Survival Guide*

Congratulations on purchasing *The Boarding School Survival Guide*! If you are reading this, you are most likely a newcomer considering applying to a boarding school, a recently admitted student trying to decide which boarding school to attend, or a current member of a boarding school community. I've been in each of those positions, and during every step of the process, I wanted to hear the authentic experiences and tips from people who had ventured down the boarding school path ahead of me.

So I embarked on a mission to write this book because it is one that I wish had been available to me throughout the application, selection, and transitional processes. Three years ago, I was a nervous middle-schooler living in a region where the concept of "boarding school" generally garners no more than a perplexed facial expression. What's more, nobody in my family had ever set foot on a boarding school campus before I thrust myself into this far-off realm. I can say with conviction that I definitely would have read every word of this book—if it had existed back then.

Since there was no good place to find answers to my incessant questions about boarding school, I instead had to find these answers myself. Though admission officers, viewbooks, and official school websites provided some informational help, I quickly realized that what I really needed was a student's perspective. After all, a promotional brochure wasn't going to tell me what to do when the dining hall serves subpar food or give me insight on navigating a dorm's communal bathroom. So I started seeking *real* advice from *real* students, and by the time I made my decision to attend Andover, I had tracked down enough current students and asked them more than enough questions to satisfy my thirst for information about boarding school (more on that in Chapter 1). Looking back, this required more effort than it should have. Until now, there has been a void of easily accessible, unsolicited information about boarding school life. But *The Boarding School Survival Guide* promises, if nothing else, anecdotal advice and useful tips about the many aspects of boarding school life from current and recently graduated students.

That said, I don't claim to be an expert on every aspect of boarding school. It's not possible, since I've only attended one boarding school and haven't even graduated yet. So I knew from the start that I needed more than just my voice to make this book successful. When I was fortunate enough to secure a publisher that believed in my project (thank you, Peterson's!), my search for other contributors began. I

1

contacted numerous heads of English departments, sought out countless editors of school newspapers, and posted incredibly frequently on Facebook and other social media sites. I appreciate the opportunity to have edited the selected students' words while striving to maintain their voices, integrity, and honesty, but I sincerely thank the hundreds of students who took the time to share their stories with me. This enthusiastic response has provided—both in terms of writers and the schools they attend—a diverse book, one composed of a wide variety of opinions and experiences that, I hope, collectively paints an accurate and truthful picture of boarding school life. This was a labor of love for my fellow contributors and me, and I hope you are able to take from it as much as we put into it. Wherever you are in the boarding school process, I wish you much success.

SCHOLARSHIP CONTEST

I didn't realize it when I was applying, but I now have a better understanding of the economic challenges of attending boarding school. For me, boarding school has been amazingly valuable in so many ways, so I want to help someone else defray the cost of this life-changing experience. I am awarding two $1,000 scholarships for deserving students to put toward their boarding school tuition. I'm delighted to be giving two lucky readers the opportunity to earn these scholarships. Please refer to the submission guidelines in the back of the book for entry instructions.

Justin Ross Muchnick
Phillips Academy Andover, Class of 2016
boardingschoolsurvival@gmail.com
April, 2014

CHAPTER 1
Boarding School:
Why I Chose This Path
and You Might, Too

by Justin Muchnick
Phillips Academy Andover—Andover, MA—Class of 2016
Hometown: Newport Beach, California

My seventh-grade literature class changed my life. To be more exact, Mr. Rogers, my seventh-grade literature teacher, changed my life. Only a temporary substitute teacher (the regular faculty member took the year off for maternity leave), Mr. Rogers entered the classroom on the first day of school and did something remarkable: he asked his students to have a conversation about a book we had read over the summer. My school's traditional "raise your hand and wait to be called on" style of learning had left me completely unprepared for a teacher who *wanted* me to talk. Nevertheless, I relished the opportunity to learn in this interesting and dynamic classroom environment, and I certainly jumped at a chance to voice my opinions without fear of being chastised for speaking out of turn.

Within a few weeks, active participation had fully cemented its reputation as the primary way of learning in Mr. Rogers's class. Instead of employing a standard row-and-column classroom seating pattern, Mr. Rogers positioned our seats in a large circle. This Harkness Method encouraged free-flowing conversations in which Mr. Rogers would serve only as a mediator and participant. Rather than writing bland responses to even blander study questions, my class honed its public speaking skills by participating in spur-of-the-moment debates about these topics. Mr. Rogers's classroom, reminiscent of a scene out of *Dead Poets Society*, allowed the act of learning to intellectually stretch and stimulate me.

3

As Mr. Rogers became my friend and mentor as well as my teacher, I learned that he had previously worked as the Writer in Residence at Phillips Exeter Academy, a boarding school in New England. At that time, I thought that boarding school was a place where disobedient children were sent to resolve their behavioral issues. Mr. Rogers, though, spoke glowingly of the East Coast boarding school system and told me that schools like Exeter utilize an active, discussion-based, Mr. Rogers-esque style of teaching. Soon, I started dreaming of a school full of teachers like Mr. Rogers, intellectually curious students, and eager learners. I did some research about Exeter and other New England schools, and in the spring of my seventh-grade year, I presented the boarding school idea to my mom and dad.

At first, my parents commended me on the excellent joke I had pulled on them; however, they quickly realized that I was serious. They began to think that I wanted to get away from them or that I disliked my family. But after extensive negotiations, I was able to convince them that this was not the case, and by midway through the summer after seventh grade, they fully backed my decision. Once my family agreed that I was in fact going to pursue the boarding school idea, we made it our mission to select the schools to which I would apply. I devised a list of qualities I was looking for in a boarding school. At this point in the application process, you, too, should create a list of criteria; you can save yourself the wasted time and effort of applying to the "wrong" schools by knowing what kinds of schools best suit you. Though your personal list may be very different, mine was as follows:

Size: I tried to find a relatively big school. At my primary school, the average grade size was about 50 students, and as time wore on, my desire to expand beyond my small group of classmates grew stronger. By applying to larger schools, I felt that I could both broaden my social experience and avoid another "small school burnout."

Uniform policy: My former school enforced a strict dress code. Since collared shirts and I never really hit if off, I decided I had definitely worn a uniform for long enough. I did not want to spend my high school years wearing a blazer and slacks.

Single-sex or coed: I didn't really want to spend my high school years at an all-boys school.

Location: For me, the East Coast seemed like the best place to find a boarding school. After all, that's what Mr. Rogers had recommended.

Academics: I have an unquenchable thirst for knowledge. I did not wish to "dehydrate" myself at a school with a less-than-excellent academic reputation.

Proximity to an airport: My mom thought of this one. She suggested that I should apply to schools located near a major airport that offered nonstop flights from Los Angeles. Cross-country flights are tough enough; complicating matters with a connecting flight seemed unnecessary.

Here are some other things that you might want to consider:

Religious affiliation: Do you want religion to play a large part in your high school experience, or would you rather go to a nondenominational school?

Specialty schools: Do you want to apply to schools that focus on a specific aspect or method of learning? Are you particularly talented in a certain field? If so, look into arts, math and sciences, or military schools.

Athletics: If you play a sport, you might try to look for schools with strong teams and adequate athletic facilities. One good way to do this is to contact a school's coach or athletic director. As both a soccer player and a wrestler, I talked to many coaches from a number of different boarding schools to get a sense of each school's athletic program.

Cost/Financial aid policy: Obviously, some schools are more expensive than others. In addition to looking at the tuition, you may want to find out which schools offer need-based financial aid or any merit-based scholarships.

By comparing various schools to my personal list of attributes, I was able to find four schools that really matched my requirements. I sent applications to Choate Rosemary Hall, The Lawrenceville School, Phillips Exeter Academy, and Phillips Academy Andover, and I was fortunate enough to have been accepted by all four. After taking the SSAT®, writing applications, and interviewing with admission officers, little did I realize that I would have one last, equally significant hurdle to jump. The choice that I was about to make would directly impact the next four years of my life, so my parents and I did everything in our power to ensure that my decision was the correct one. By obtaining contact information from admission offices as well as school counselors and friends of friends, we sought out current students who lived locally and attended each of the schools. We scheduled face-to-face meetings with as many of them as we could, during which we "grilled" them on the pros and cons of their schools. We spent hours reading websites, blogs, and Facebook pages in hopes of getting students' unsolicited perspectives of their schools (and just as many hours searching for a book like this!). Most importantly, however, we attended the revisit days for each of the schools. For those at this stage of the boarding school process, I would highly recommend going to the admitted students events if you have the financial means and your schedule permits. At any given revisit day, I was truly able to get a feel for the campus and environment and see if I could envision myself as a student at that school next year—sometimes my gut instinct would tell me "yes," and other times it would tell me "no." While on campus, I also had the opportunity to ask countless current students about their high school experiences. Don't be afraid to ask tough questions. By doing so, you can better understand the general campus vibe. After the revisit days, I was able to make my decision with confidence. I was going to Andover!

You might choose to apply to boarding schools for different reasons than I did. No two cases are exactly alike, but many applicants fall into these categories.

Ready to leave home: Whether it's a desire for independence, friction within the household, or any other reason, waiting until college to live on your own isn't the best option for you.

Family tradition: As a baby, you wore a boarding school bib around your neck. Your favorite shirt is one emblazoned with a particular school's emblem. A few older family members have paved the way, or, perhaps generations of relatives have attended. Boarding school is in your blood.

Searching for diversity: You have grown up in a homogenous community, or you yearn for difference, in both tradition and mindset. Today's boarding schools afford you interaction with peers of all racial, financial, geographical, and religious backgrounds—conducive to a multicultural educational experience.

Love of learning: Is your nose perpetually stuck in a book? Do you stay after class to delve deeper into a conversation with your teacher? Is your idea of a fun weekend activity reading up on political affairs or the latest scientific breakthrough? Do you love learning for learning's sake? If so, boarding school is undoubtedly worth exploring.

For me, the process of applying to and selecting boarding schools was fueled by my innate passion for learning: I simply wanted to find a place where it was cool to be smart. When I look back at this initial notion, I realize that it was certainly idealistic and a bit naïve, but Andover has come about as close as possible. Though busy work and uninteresting conversations bog me down from time to time, they are more than made up for by engaging writing prompts, stimulating discussions, and inspirational teachers who would make even Mr. Rogers proud.

ABOUT JUSTIN MUCHNICK

At Phillips Academy Andover, I am captain of the varsity wrestling team, play soccer, participate in the chess club, and work as a campus tour guide. I am the co-author of *Straight-A Study Skills* (Adams Media, January, 2013) and had an essay about boarding school published in *Peterson's 2014–15 Private Secondary Schools* guide. I am also a journalist for *The Bootleg* (www.scout.com), Stanford University's sports news website, where I publish articles about college football. Recently I became the youngest charter content creator for Yoursports.com, a social publishing platform for sports. My academic interests include reading, writing, Latin, and modern American history. When I am not at boarding school, I live with my three younger siblings (Jacob, Ross, and Ally) and my parents. I'm an avid fan of *Star Wars* and *Rocky,* and I recently became addicted to the P90X workout DVDs.

CHAPTER 2
Applying to Boarding School: Essays, Interviews, and More

by Alexandra Willcutt
Baylor School—Chattanooga, Tennessee—Class of 2018
Hometown: Lexington, Kentucky

Applying to boarding school can be quite intimidating. It is definitely nerve-wracking for an eighth grader to take the SSAT®, write application essays, visit schools, and perform well in an interview. But these tips can make the application process much less stressful.

MAKING YOUR LIST OF SCHOOLS

First, decide which schools you are going to apply to. Here's how I started. I printed out a list of all the boarding schools in the country along with their location, attendance by gender, and size. I started by crossing off the ones that were too far away (distance from home was important to my mom and me). Next, I went through and eliminated schools because of their attendance by gender; I wanted to go to a coed school, so that ruled out schools that were single-sex. Then, I eliminated schools based on their size, since I didn't want a school that was too small or too large for my liking. You might have other athletic, academic, or social wants and needs. Whittle down your list accordingly.

TAKING STANDARDIZED TESTS

The next step after making a list of boarding schools that fit your preferences is to take the Secondary School Admission Test (SSAT). I was very nervous about taking the SSAT, since I knew that a bad score could be highly detrimental. In fact, I was so anxious that I studied and did practice tests over the summer and on all of my weekends and breaks leading up to the test date. I utilized online practice tests, but the most helpful tool I used was a book called The Princeton Review's *Cracking the SSAT & ISEE*. Of course, there are other test-prep books that you can order online or check out at the library, and any will do a good job of preparing you for the test. Some of my friends have used tutors or test-prep classes to help prepare for the SSAT. As long as you are practicing in some way, you are preparing for the test.

On the day of the SSAT, I entered the room with several other students. I had brought a couple of sharpened #2 pencils, a water bottle, and a few snacks. I sat in my seat confidently and waited for the writing sample booklet to be passed out. For me, this was the hardest section of the test, not because I don't like writing or that I'm not good at it, but mainly because I am a slow writer. After the 25 minutes of writing, I finished the rest of the test—2 hours and 35 minutes of math, reading comprehension, and vocabulary. When I finished, I left the room confident that I had done well.

Later, when my SSAT scores arrived, I found out I didn't do as well as I had expected. If this happens to you, don't despair! There will probably be another test in your area sometime soon; just sign up for that one and be ready to ace it! Luckily for me, another test was being held a few months later. I continued studying and tried to learn from my errors on the last test. I did everything just like I had before, but this time with a little more knowledge and extra preparation. When I received my second SSAT scores, I was happy to see that I had done much better.

Another test that many boarding schools accept in lieu of (or in addition to) the SSAT is the Independent School Entrance Exam (ISEE®). The test itself is very similar in both content and format to the SSAT. If you attend an independent grade school, check with your current school's counselor to find out if the ISEE is administered at your school. Many private schools offer this test internally. If this is the case for you, it would be wise to compare your scores on the ISEE with those of the SSAT.

Note: If you are an international student, read Chapter 23 for more about the Test of English as a Foreign Language (TOEFL).

GETTING TEACHER RECOMMENDATIONS

The SSAT is only the first step of the process of applying to boarding school. Next come the teacher recommendations and application forms. Most schools request a recommendation letter from your English and math teachers, so make sure that you've built strong relationships with these teachers so that they can write recommendations that accurately describe you as a student and person.

Some schools also require one or two recommendation letters from other people who know you well. While usually teachers, this could be another mentor, coach, or adult advisor or counselor who knows you well. Also, don't forget to send a heartfelt thank-you note to anyone who wrote a letter of recommendation for you. Your teachers took time out of their busy lives to do something nice for you, so let them know that you appreciate their work on your behalf.

CREATING YOUR STUDENT RÉSUMÉ

Next, I went to work creating my résumé and filling out the rest of the application form. Building a résumé is quite simple; you just need to write a list of the things you have accomplished or done in your middle school years. I listed the sports I had participated in (in addition to any athletic awards or distinctions I had won), my academic achievements, and any extracurricular activities like Girl Scouts and community service. I also included any interesting summer experiences and jobs as well as some of my hobbies and interests.

WRITING ESSAYS

Create online application profiles for yourself at each school you want to apply to so you know what essay questions each school requires. Some schools share an online Common Application form, while others have individual applications for their schools. For example, The Association of Boarding Schools (TABS) provides a form that over 200 boarding schools accept, and The Gateway to Prep Schools has forty schools that subscribe to their forms. Check to see which application forms the schools on your list use.

Look at the essay prompts from your schools. Some schools let you answer their questions online, while others require you to write them on a form. I typed my answers in a word-processing program to create a rough draft and continued editing them until I finally submitted the final drafts online or by hand (depending on the school).

Some questions are straightforward and simple, but others require more thought. No matter what, be sincere and honest—and make sure to check for spelling, grammatical, and mechanical errors! Understand that this is a chance for your "voice" to be heard on paper, and give your reader a glimpse of who you are. Share personal anecdotes and experiences that convey the way you think, interact, and see yourself in this world. Use examples to illustrate your points, and write in the first person. Feel free to be humorous, serious, or somewhere in between, but remember to share who you are. Finally, don't forget to do your homework on each school. If the application asks why you want to attend there, be sure you have concrete examples of why that school is unique or appeals to you.

VISITING SCHOOLS

After submitting all the components of my written application, I had to make a good impression on the admission officers and the school community. Almost all boarding schools have some form of campus visit and tour, and some offer an overnight visit program. These are good opportunities to meet students and faculty and are also a great way to get a feel for what campus life is like. By shadowing a student or taking a student-guided tour, you can see the school from a student's perspective. You should also use this as a chance to ask your student host questions like these:

- What's your favorite thing to do on campus on the weekends?
- How often do you leave campus on the weekends?
- What are your favorite and least favorite classes?
- Is there lots of "drama" on campus?
- What is your favorite campus tradition?
- Do many students get in trouble, and what is it usually for?
- How is the cafeteria food?
- Do you like the school?

Note: More details on campus visits can be found in Chapter 6.

PREPARING FOR AN INTERVIEW

When visiting a school, you will have an interview. If you don't visit a school's campus, you should contact an admission officer via e-mail. This officer will put you in touch with a colleague or alumnus, and you will have an opportunity to interview either in person or through Skype or video chat. I was so nervous about the interview that I thought of possible questions I might be asked and came up with my answers a couple of days before interviewing. This worked very well, especially with particularly tough questions, because I already had a rough idea of what I was going to say.

Note: Some helpful sample interview questions can be found in Chapter 6.

Using these tips might make applying to boarding school a little less daunting for you. Hopefully, you should now be ready to breeze through your applications! Best of luck!

ABOUT ALEXANDRA WILLCUTT

I am creative and I love to take pictures, read good books, and listen to a wide variety of alternative, indie, and classic rock music. You can also find me writing, drawing, or just thinking. I come from a rather large family in Kentucky, with three sisters, one brother, and an assortment of different pets. My favorite subjects are English, art, science, and French.

CHAPTER 3
Financial Aid:
Paying for Boarding School

by Deanna Havey
Phillips Exeter Academy—Exeter, New Hampshire—Class of 2014
Hometown: Amesbury, Massachusetts

If you're considering applying for boarding school but are concerned that the price tag could be an obstacle, don't let finances stop you. Being a financial aid candidate may require more paperwork, but it doesn't mean you have to rule out boarding school altogether.

Just like with colleges, the big-name boarding schools offer some of the best financial aid. But with some online research, you can find plenty of other schools that also have sizable financial aid budgets. Each school has its own endowment and policies, so you should look for specific tuition and aid information on each school's website. Phrases like "meets full demonstrated need" or "need-blind" may indicate a school with a good financial aid record. If the website doesn't provide that information, you can always call the school and ask. You might also want to find out whether financial aid awards can be used to cover books, school supplies, flights to and from home, or other expenditures; if the aid package changes annually; if there are academic conditions tied to the financial aid; and if the school offers any work-study options.

Exeter offers a type of work-study option where students are paid New Hampshire's minimum wage. We only need to fill out a single tax form to be employed, and there's a limit of 6 hours per week. In addition, any student, regardless of whether he or she receives financial aid, can take paid proctoring jobs in different venues across campus. Students can proctor in the library checking out books or in the computer lab lending a hand with technology problems. A friend of mine even proctors in the ceramics studio. In the past three years, I've proctored in both the music library and the computer lab, and I recently was promoted to head proctor of the computer lab. For me, it's great to be able to use a free block or two every week for proctoring and make a little money for school supplies or spending.

At most boarding schools there are usually students from a range of financial backgrounds. Some kids worry that being a financial aid student at a boarding school will put them at a social disadvantage. First of all, no one will know unless you announce it. The names of financial aid recipients are kept quite confidential no matter what school you attend. Second, there isn't a noticeable difference in social dynamics. No one should think any less of you because of where you come from, geographically or financially. However, it can be hard for people who have lived on a tight budget their whole lives to get accustomed to living with some students who aren't so financially conscious. At Exeter, students tend to do a lot of online shopping, and for some it's not a big deal to drop a couple hundred dollars on a single item. Another time when the uneven financial playing field may become a minor issue is right after school vacation, when kids share stories about what they did over break. A few classmates may recount their third trip to Europe, while others have never even had the opportunity to fly to a vacation destination because of their family's financial situation. It's a common occurrence, but try to understand that more privileged students aren't trying to brag—just take their accounts of exotic trips as opportunities to learn about different experiences and cultures around the world! (And if you are fortunate enough to come from an advantageous financial background, try to be sensitive to the fact that some of your peers aren't in the same position.)

THE PROCESS

Financial aid applications are usually due around the same time as your admission application, and it is very important that the deadlines are adhered to strictly. Requests for financial aid will not be considered after admission decisions. Generally, a financial aid application will consist of a Parents' Financial Statement (PFS), a copy of an income-verification document such as a federal tax return, and copies of your W-2 forms (or 1099s, if applicable). These are submitted to School & Student Services (SSS) for processing. The SSS objectively calculates an estimate of what your family can afford for tuition. When schools say financial aid will be determined by "demonstrated financial need," the estimate determined by SSS is what they mean.

Many factors will come into play when the SSS assesses a family's financial situation: the household's income, the value of any assets, banking accounts, any major debts, the size of the family, and how many school tuitions the family is currently paying. Other factors may include a recent divorce or job loss. More specific information on how financial aid is determined can be found online in *The SSS Family Guide to Financial Aid.* Your family might also consider a loan to supplement your financial aid package.

Most of the time, schools do not select students on a need-blind basis, and financial aid candidates are put in a separate and often larger admissions pool. A student who qualifies for financial aid isn't always guaranteed aid; unfortunately, the number of financial aid applicants often exceeds the available aid. But don't let that deter you from applying for financial aid, since the candidate pool and amount of aid available changes from year to year.

ADDITIONAL SCHOLARSHIPS

Today, almost anything can be found online with a search engine, and this includes boarding school scholarships. If your family isn't granted the financial aid package you were hoping for, there are a few outside options for funding. You can Google "private school scholarships" and the name of your state to find scholarship sources. Additional well-known scholarship sources include the Jack Kent Cooke Foundation, Admission Quest, your local Rotary Clubs, and Be A Prep Kid.

For links to these and other useful resources, see Useful Resources for Boarding School Students at the back of this book.

Best of luck with the financial aid process. Education is truly a worthwhile investment.

ABOUT DEANNA HAVEY

I am a day student at Exeter, and my education has been made possible by a generous financial aid scholarship provided by the academy. I'm grateful for the opportunities it has presented to me. Biology and chemistry are my favorite subjects, so this year I'll be taking molecular genetics and a biology research course. In the future, I hope to pursue a career in a STEM field. In addition to my academic work, I've been able to try cool activities at school such as fencing, crew, and archery. I participate in the dance, environmental, and engineering clubs. My senior year, I will be Head Proctor of my job on campus. Outside of school, I am an active member of my church community and compete in an advanced tap dance company in Amesbury, Massachusetts.

CHAPTER 4
Single-Sex Boarding School:
Is It for You?

by Kelsey Burns
Miss Porter's School—Farmington, Connecticut—Class of 2012
Hometown: Horsham, Pennsylvania

N o, I did not wear a plaid skirt every day. No, my classmates were not all lesbians. Yes, we did shave our legs regularly. Yes, I know how to talk to guys and have male friends. Yes, we had sports teams. Yes, there was a boys' school nearby. Yes, I did go on dates during high school.

When I tell people that I went to an all-girls boarding school, I find myself answering the same questions. It's hard not to roll my eyes at this point. Once we get through what I consider to be the formalities, I generally get asked two questions. The first is: "Did you like it?" Yes. I wouldn't have traded my time there for the world.

The single-sex education I received was not a remnant of an antiquated past, a school clinging to outdated ideas of one gender being better suited to one environment or another. Instead, it focused on fostering an environment that allowed my classmates and me to fully explore what it meant to be an individual without the hindrances of gender roles. At Miss Porter's, girls dominated the math and science fields. In fact, girls dominated every field. And our brother school had both a prized football team as well as a prized theater department. There was never any pressure to find interests in certain areas based on conforming to gender stereotypes; you were only expected to fully develop yourself in whatever way that felt right.

I believe that, as a result, the majority of my classmates became very confident young women. They are now able to go into the world and command the respect they deserve. They are going to be the voices of the future. These are the women who will go forth and close the wage gap, be the president, find new sources of clean energy, feed the hungry, and cure cancer. These are the women who will go and do everything, simply because they were given the chance to do everything. What single-sex education, and especially single-sex boarding, sets out to teach you is that your gender does not define what fields you will and will not be competent in.

And while I didn't know it at age 14, all of this answers the second and more difficult question I get asked: "Why did you choose to go to an all-girls school?" If you choose to go to a single-sex school, you will forever be challenged to defend that choice. The good news is that it is a choice worth defending. The bad news is that no matter how many success stories and statistics you pull out, some people will always think you missed out on something.

So what did I miss out on? Well, we didn't have a football team or cheerleaders. Still, I can't really say that I missed out because many girls attended football games at one of the nearby all-boys schools (although I guess there were still no cheerleaders). During the week, while I was in classes, I didn't feel the absence of boys. The absence of boys was only noticeable during the occasional class discussions when I found myself thinking, "What would a guy think about this character's actions? Would he find them natural or justifiable?" or, "I wonder how men's lives would be affected by this law we're discussing?" But, in fact, because healthy conversation and debate comes from having various opinions represented, my school created a special class in conjunction with one of our brother schools, Avon Old Farms, where students came together to discuss contemporary social issues.

The only times I really ever missed having guys around was on the weekends. When it came time to just hang out, it's sometimes nice to vary the tone of your social groups—not to mention there are certain social hallmarks of coed schools that are hard to adapt for a single-sex environment. Alas, my dreams of being on the homecoming court were crushed. I did actually go to homecoming (twice) with public school friends. At Miss Porter's, though, we even had a prom! Granted, our dates were what we jokingly referred to as "imports" because they came from back home, the brother schools, the local public school, or, in some cases, happened to be a friend's sibling. My point is that socially, going to a single-sex school only limits you if you let it. Much like going to any school, you should reach out to people beyond your immediate community, and maintain past connections while building new friendships.

Despite this, you may never be as close to some of the people outside of the school community as you are to those who are in the fold. One of the most amazing things about boarding school is how close you get to be with all of your friends. I think this is doubly true with single-sex schools. Being a student at an all-girls school means the bonds you form transcend the "club member" feeling and are instead closer to that of a large extended family. I often find myself referencing someone I went to school with, usually someone I didn't think I was particularly close with, and I say, "Oh, I had a friend from high school who . . ." Everyone is automatically a friend, and the people you are close to are so much more than that.

There are a couple of things specific to single-sex schools that really foster this closeness. For starters, single-sex schools are generally very small. At my school you would have had to try really hard not to know every student's name and at least one fact about her. These schools also tend to be tied very closely to their traditions. There are certain things that simply become hallmarks of student life and become a common bond with every other student currently in the school, as well as anyone else who has ever studied within those hallowed halls. You learn to speak the language of the students and treasure the quirks of student life. At my school, for example, we fondly call our alumnae "Ancients." On more occasions than I can count, I've had other Ancients approach me on the streets upon catching a glimpse of my school apparel simply to gush about their own experiences and relive them vicariously through mine. It is universally understood that any Ancient (no matter where in the world you find her) is a friend and a connection to be treasured.

Another aspect of single-sex boarding school is the focus on community. The word "community" was probably used at least once every day in classes, assemblies, or at sit-down dinners from the day I arrived on campus until the day I graduated. We had activities geared toward community building, and we were often brought together to face problems as a single body. It was very clear to me that building a cooperative, accepting, and happy group of people was as much a goal as producing strong academic and athletic results.

And of course, I do have to acknowledge the fact that one of the major sources of jealousy and stress in a teenage girl's life was removed—yes, boys, I'm talking about you! I distinctly remember a situation in my freshman year that involved a friend of mine sobbing her eyes out until two in the morning because of a dance where another girl had better luck with a boy that my friend liked. The following days involved the first girl sprinting out of the dining hall or off to another building every time she saw the second girl walk in. It was all very comical, and fortunately, they made peace within the week. Based on that scenario, I am positive that many of us were a good deal happier without boys around all of the time (which isn't to say that we didn't still think about them a lot of the time!).

Finally, I cannot overstate the sense of comfort derived from being around people who specialized in the issues that most immediately impact your life. Everywhere I turned there was information on things pertinent to me and my life: Workshops on women in the workplace? Check. Lectures on women's mental health and physical fitness? Check. Coaches trained to work with women's bodies for the best results? Check. Beyond simply having information readily available, there were also role models for students to look to and learn from every day. We were regularly addressed by successful women from all fields who offered fantastic insight and inspiration.

At every boarding school, you form unusually close relationships with the faculty. During my high school years, many faculty members took on the roles of mothers, fathers, aunts, and uncles. They doled out advice, comfort, reality checks, and plenty of snacks! They are lifelong mentors and confidants who offer more wisdom and understanding than you'll ever fully appreciate during your time together. Now I look back and realize how much I learned from just being around them.

In addition, inspiration abounds among your fellow students. Almost all of my classmates held some sort of leadership position throughout their time at the school. I think this is one of the most amazing aspects of having gone to an all-girls school. Girls automatically have the experience of being responsible and accountable for something, of being able to make decisions and face consequences. They build critical personal and professional skills and are therefore more prepared to take positions in the working world.

To be fair, each student takes away something different from her time at an all-girls school. Before Miss Porter's, some of my classmates felt too shy in class to speak up or answer questions. Some were uncomfortable with their bodies and therefore wouldn't try new sports. Some didn't know how to express their competence and desire for respect from their peers and elders. Some of us (read: me) thought (and were wrong) that we didn't have much to learn from a girls' school. And all of us learned different things that we take into the wider world. But we all learned something, and we all learned it together. This is why I think that single-sex education is a beautiful, relevant, and exciting opportunity that you should strongly consider!

ABOUT KELSEY BURNS

At Miss Porter's, I was captain of the debate team, head of school spirit, editor of the newspaper's opinion page, head of the Republican Club, and a member of the varsity diving and softball teams. After graduation, I coached a summer diving program in New York. In college, I took up sailing in order to stay active, and I now enjoy sailing with my boarding school friends. I fondly remember my years at Miss Porter's, and I frequently volunteer for the school. Given how positive my boarding school experience was, I wish all future boarding school students an equally happy one.

CHAPTER 5
Specialized Boarding Schools:
Why I Attended an Arts School

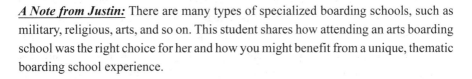

by Katie Watson
Interlochen Arts Academy—Interlochen, Michigan—Class of 2013
Hometown: Los Angeles, California

A Note from Justin: There are many types of specialized boarding schools, such as military, religious, arts, and so on. This student shares how attending an arts boarding school was the right choice for her and how you might benefit from a unique, thematic boarding school experience.

I am, and have always been, a nervous wreck with an unquenchable thirst for adventure. Due to the contradictory nature of these two traits, I often throw myself into situations that cause me anxiety. One such situation was begging my family to let me enroll at an arts-based boarding school.

My background is largely academic. I excelled throughout middle school; my freshman year of high school was spent at a small, academically rigorous magnet school. At first I felt that the school was a perfect fit—a tight-knit campus of future engineers, doctors, and lawyers. But as the year progressed, I began to see the cracks in its perfection.

As an avid painter, I was astounded by the total lack of art in my school curriculum. To remedy the zero hours of art class at school, I took 6 hours of art every Saturday at the local arts college, creating an elective six-day school week. I knew, however, that I wouldn't have the time to do this during sophomore year due to a crazier schedule. This was unacceptable to me, and I came to realize that, while I loved the academic aspect of my current school, I could not be happy if it prevented my pursuit of an artistic education.

This small realization spiraled quickly into deeper, darker questions of whether I wanted to seriously consider attending an arts school. I felt incomplete without my art classes. I threw myself into researching different schools, particularly local art-magnet schools. Boarding schools weren't originally part of my vision, but I became increasingly discouraged by the low-quality academics at local arts high schools. I wanted a balance between my academic and artistic pursuits. I wanted them to be equally strong.

I don't remember how I heard about Interlochen, but I do remember devouring every web page and booklet of information I could find about it. With each moment spent reading about this school I became more excited, as it was the first school that fit the structure I wanted. That spring of freshman year was a blur of paperwork and phone calls. Looking back, deciding to apply was one of the best decisions I've made.

WHAT IS AN ARTS BOARDING SCHOOL?

The main difference between an arts boarding school and a traditional college-prep boarding school is the inclusion of artistic majors in the curriculum. Such majors include creative writing, dance, motion picture arts, music, theater, and visual arts. Instead of applying directly to the school, you apply to a specific arts department within the school. Once you become an accepted member of that department, a large chunk of your schedule is spent in courses dedicated to your major. For example, if you're majoring in visual arts, you might take four academic classes and four arts classes. Thus your semester classes might include English, science, foreign language, math, painting, sculpture, ceramics, and photography.

However, the arts emphasis doesn't end there. Art usually finds its way into academic coursework—you might find musical notation being used as a metaphor in calculus or a student choreographing a short dance for a chemistry project. Walking through campus, you can hear the sound of violins seeping through practice room walls, mixing with Broadway tunes being belted from second-story dorm rooms. Art is not an addition; it is deeply integrated into every aspect of campus life.

WHO BENEFITS FROM AN ARTS-BASED CURRICULUM?

In my opinion, everyone benefits. Those planning to pursue artistic fields, of course, benefit immensely. Generally, students who develop their artistic skills in an intense pre-collegiate environment prepare themselves for further artistic success. At an arts school, it isn't uncommon to be congratulating three kids in your 12-person English class on their acceptances to Juilliard.

But regardless of what you choose to pursue after high school, you will definitely benefit from arts school if art in any form interests you. Before attending Interlochen, I was overwhelmed by the choice between a traditional school and an arts school. I was completely freaking out over what direction I wanted to take. At the time, my preference towards the arts led me to attend Interlochen. However, when it was time to go to college, I decided to attend a traditional university rather than an arts school.

So, I'm going to present you with the question that I've been asked on many occasions:

Knowing what I know now that I'm attending a traditional college, if I could go back in time, would I have chosen to remain at a traditional high school? The answer is, without a doubt, NO.

In college, I will not have the time for the in-depth arts study that I had for the past three years. As a freshman, I will be working to fulfill all of the required credits for graduation; my summers will be busy with internships and summer jobs. While I may be able to justify taking an art class here and there, the reality is that I won't be spending every minute in the art studios. While I'm a bit saddened by this (I've gotten used to spending hours upon hours in the painting studio), I am not heartbroken. And that is because I'm soothed by how much I've learned in the past few years. I feel confident in my abilities to continue my artistic practice independently.

Having the opportunity to take a few years to study a passion in-depth, with no repercussions, is one I feel all should pursue. If you're an artist in any sense of the word, I beg you to at least consider attending an arts boarding school.

WHAT ARE ACADEMICS LIKE AT AN ARTS SCHOOL?

The rigor of academics at an arts school depends on what you are seeking. It is totally feasible to have a not-so-rigorous academic schedule, if that's what you want. There are many students who choose to fill their schedules with art classes rather than academics. However, if you are more academically inclined, it is possible to shift your schedule in that direction. I split my schedule evenly: 4 hours of art and 4 hours of academics per day.

To be honest, the science and math classes at Interlochen weren't as challenging as those at my old school. But it wasn't for lack of great teachers. If you find that the course is moving too slowly, there is ample opportunity for advanced study. For example, the pre-calculus class I was enrolled in during the first semester of my sophomore year was covering concepts I already knew. After I talked to my teacher, he agreed that during the second semester I could take an independent study course in discrete mathematics, a field in which I'd be more intellectually stimulated. It was a great course and a wonderful opportunity. On the flipside, I've found that the liberal arts courses are exceptionally strong. The literature courses I took at Interlochen were easily some of the best classes I've had within my educational career.

WHO SHOULDN'T ATTEND AN ARTS SCHOOL?

An arts school is certainly not for everyone. The following are my lists of those who shouldn't—and should—attend an arts boarding school:

- **Students with absolutely no interest in the arts.**
- **Students interested in pursuing athletics.** There are no organized sports teams due to the small campus size and absence of student athletes. If participating in sports is an important part of your life, you might be happier at a school with more athletic facilities.
- **Those uncomfortable with social liberalism.** Arts schools tend to be very liberal. If you are socially conservative and want to attend an arts-based school, you definitely should consider it, but be aware that you might be more alone in your political views.
- **Those who aren't willing to put in a lot of time and effort to hone their artistic craft.** You are worked to the bone and it feels so good. But seriously, you will likely have a very heavy artistic workload, so if you want a calmer schedule, an arts-based school might not be a good fit.
- **Those uncomfortable with small campuses and more rural locations.** Speaking as a girl from a big city, this really isn't as big a deal as you might think. But if rural environments really aren't your thing, you might want to look elsewhere.
- **Students who want to attend certain schools like Oxford, Cambridge, or Caltech.** I know that might seem like an odd trio, but it's due to the nature of their admissions processes. Oxford, Cambridge, Caltech, and some other schools are very objective when sorting through applications, with admissions criteria heavily focused on academic rigor and GPA. Attending an arts school makes it a bit more difficult, though not impossible, to fulfill requirements for admission. However, I do feel MIT is in reach for engineering-oriented arts students.

WHO SHOULD ATTEND AN ARTS SCHOOL?

- **Students who want to attend virtually any other college.** Some of the colleges that students from my rather small graduating class chose to attend are Berklee College of Music, Boston University, Carnegie Mellon University (for theater), Columbia University–Juilliard School (dual degree), Curtis Institute of Music, Harvard University, Juilliard School Dance Division, Juilliard School Music Division, NYU, Princeton University, Rhode Island School of Design, Royal Scottish Academy, Stanford University, UCLA, University of Michigan, USC, and Wesleyan University. I matriculated to Yale University, my dream school. Thus, if you want to attend an arts boarding school, but are worried that it will jeopardize your chances at college admissions, relax. Universities usually appreciate students with unique life paths, and attending an arts boarding school can actually work to your benefit by setting you apart from other academically inclined students.

- **Those who love the arts.** I guess this should go without saying.

THE APPLICATION PROCESS

Once you've decided that you want to attend an arts boarding school, do some research to find out which one(s) you'd like to attend. There are three arts boarding schools in the United States: Interlochen Arts Academy (Interlochen, Michigan), Idyllwild Arts Academy (Idyllwild, California), and Walnut Hill School for the Arts (Natick, Massachusetts). Choosing the right school is a very personal decision. If you can visit them, I highly recommend it, but if they're too far away, you can explore every page of their websites and do other research. I chose to attend Interlochen even before setting foot on campus, purely from conversations with current students and reading all of the material I could find about the school.

Next, you have to figure out which department holds the most interest for you. Each department has its own application criteria, usually a short essay and a portfolio or audition.

APPLICATION ADVICE BY MAJOR

The following is advice from students who majored in the arts—what they recommend for your application to an arts boarding school.

Creative Writing

"I would say that, in general, showcasing one's ability to write (technically, grammatically, formally, and so on) is not nearly as important as the strength and commitment of one's rhetoric."

~ E.K., creative writer, 2014 graduate

Dance

"When applying for dance, it is crucial to remember that admission officers are looking for something or someone that excites them. Whether this means someone with the perfect feet or someone with the most unique or unusual way of moving, they are looking for someone they will be invested in helping. In addition to being exciting, they also want to see a hard worker. How you can show that in a short audition is something that you must think about before going in."

~ J.G., dancer, 2013 graduate

Motion Picture Arts (MPA)

"The MPA department is looking for passionate individuals with demonstrated work ethic. It doesn't matter if you've never done film before, though prior experience is obviously a plus. They're looking for people who want to work, learn, and fall in love with the art form."

~ C.A., Motion Picture Arts major, 2013 graduate

Music

"For music, I think the most important thing to remember when applying and auditioning is that they aren't looking for perfection, because in music, you're never a finished product. But what they want is someone who has a great attitude and is willing to learn."

~ S.C., bass player, 2013 graduate

Theater

"I would recommend students auditioning for theater to be prepared and practice a lot because that is the only thing you can control in an audition. You can't make the teachers like you or guess what each teacher appreciates in a person and try to be that. But if you love the piece that you are presenting, and if you practiced it well and took the time to understand it, you will feel confident performing it. And whether you get in or not, you will know that you did the best that you can do and probably learned something wonderful from the experience."

~ M.K., theater major, 2013 graduate

Visual Arts

"When applying to the arts department, it's a matter of being open to approaching art from different avenues than you may be used to. In terms of your portfolio, it's best to have as much life drawing as possible, as well as any conceptual pieces you might have. Leave out drawings of eyes, celebrities, and models. The art teachers often look less at your portfolio and more at your potential. They truly desire students who are excited by and have a genuine love for the visual arts."

~Me

A SUMMARY OF MY EXPERIENCE

On my first day as a student at Interlochen, I was greeted by dorms, practice studios, art buildings, cafeterias, and performance venues. Registration took place in a narrow hallway of seemingly endless booths and paperwork. Returning students ran down the hall, catapulting themselves into each other's arms. New students moved carefully from booth to booth, filling out health forms and insuring their instruments. I picked up my dorm room assignment (Mozart-Beethoven first floor) and began the tasks of any new boarding school student: unpacking, roommate conversations, exploring, socializing, panicking at the realization you're at boarding school, and more unpacking.

That first week was a blur of meetings. There was an unending stream of topics prompting discussion: campus rules, dorm life, schedules, emergency procedures, roommate agreements. I was somewhat overwhelmed as I attempted to adjust to life away from home. I tried on emotions as if they were accessories or shades of lipstick. I don't remember the individual days, just the anxiety that hung over me like a cloud. However, I can, with absolute clarity, recall the moment everything clicked.

It was the evening I became fully enchanted with the school. It was at the first coffeehouse of the year, an open-mic event hosted and performed by my peers. There must have been at least 70 students crammed into the small, dark building. A third of the students were seated in metal chairs; the rest of us stood pressed together in the small space between the chairs and the back wall. Christmas lights stretched across furniture and walls, and the three hosts (older, returning students) sat on a ragged couch in the front of the room. One approached the mic and began to introduce the various acts. Students dragged guitars and each other up to the front. Even though my legs were tired, I stood transfixed. The talent in that room should have set it ablaze. Somewhat familiar faces created effortless jazz and original ballads. There was laughter, joy, and above all, community. That was the night I fell in love with my school.

Of course, time moves on. As seasons passed I became increasingly comfortable, school became home, and home became a second life. The one constant over the three years, despite graduations and new students, was the music—metaphorically and literally—of campus life.

ABOUT KATIE WATSON

I have lived in Los Angeles for four years, but I grew up in one of the many suburban valleys on the outskirts of the city. My desire to attend boarding school was a result of my stubborn independence and a desire for a strong arts education. My first year I was woefully unprepared for a Michigan winter. (Tip: If you take morning showers, your hair WILL freeze the moment you leave your dorm!) When not staying up all night to write chemistry lab reports, I can be found painting, backpacking, and watching mountaineering documentaries. While I've matriculated at Yale, I've decided to take a gap year—most of which will be spent backpacking across Peru and worrying my poor parents.

CHAPTER 6
Campus Visits:
Walking in Their Shoes

by Sophia Clarke
Pomfret School—Pomfret, Connecticut—Class of 2015
Hometown: Boston, Massachusetts

So you've decided to apply to boarding school—what's next? You need to set a date for your first campus visit. Up to this point, all you may have seen of the school are impressive pictures of diverse students studying together on luscious green grass or eating with faculty members under flags of many nations. Now the big day has finally come when you are going to walk on that same grass and feel a little bit like the students in the glossy viewbooks that you have been thumbing through for weeks. While on your tour you might see that passionate drama student from the brochure in her calculus class, or the athletic prodigy from Nigeria learning Spanish. A campus visit is when the school stops being just images on a web page and comes alive. While your mom may be fussing over what you should wear, there are far more important things for you to think about before you visit any campus.

By now, you've probably learned the importance of doing your schoolwork completely and finishing it on time. This same diligence applies to the boarding school selection process. Study the website, viewbooks, and information guides about the schools you have decided to visit. Often one ivy-covered building, impressive library, or athletic field can blend into another, creating a blurred, "Harry Potter" mash-up of all the boarding schools that you're visiting. Know the differences between the schools' offerings before you arrive. If you're interested in a particular sport or extracurricular activity, be sure to get in touch with a coach or instructor before you even set foot on a venerable old cobblestone. This lets the admission office know that you have sincere interest in the school's specifics and also shows that you've done your research!

In addition, be sure to know the school's dress code, motto, and mission statement. Being familiar with the dress code before visiting a campus is very important. Nobody likes to feel underdressed or overdressed, and these fashion faux pas are also the most obvious way for a visitor to feel disengaged from an already-established community. Make sure that you are wearing weather-appropriate clothes, and be slightly dressed up. Not only will you look sharp, but you will feel sharp, too. Also, the school's mission statement and motto should be on your mind while touring and interviewing at the school. Admission officers will be impressed that you are aware of their school's mantras or credos.

The night before a campus visit, go to bed at a reasonable hour and set your alarm. Have your appropriate outfit laid out or ready to go in your closet. Make sure that your outfit brings out your personality. Accessorize with a cute headband or bowtie if you so desire, but don't go overboard on the eye makeup or cologne.

Remember to have a map printed out or a GPS navigator set for the easiest and most time-efficient way to get to the school. I cannot overstate how important it is to get off at the right exit when driving to a campus. Most boarding schools are in small towns, and it takes a lot of stress off you and your parents to know where you are going.

Here's why I emphasize having accurate directions and plenty of driving time. One of the schools I was considering hosted prospective families for a day. The itinerary included a student panel, campus tour, interview, and lunch with the faculty. The event began at eight in the morning, so my parents and I left home at 7 a.m. to ensure that we would arrive on campus with a few minutes to spare. On our way to the seaside school, we realized that our car needed oil. We stopped by a local auto shop to have it checked out. The oil change was fast and easy, but a small hinge on the front of the car wouldn't latch onto the hood. For the next 30 minutes, the garage staff wrestled the car's hood down with the help of a bungee cord. Needless to say, we arrived late—the only positive was that it made for a good ice-breaker during the interview!

So let's assume that you've arrived on time. Now, be sure to shake hands with your tour guide and interviewer, refrain from chewing gum, and look excited! Good old-fashioned manners go a long way, especially when you are making a first impression.

The campus tour is usually the first activity. Your tour guide will generally be a student. Many times, these students volunteer their free blocks to take prospective families on a tour, and they are very excited to show you their school community. Don't be afraid to ask them any questions you might have. Remember, they were once taking tours themselves, so they've been in your shoes. The best questions are those that aren't easily answered by looking at the school's website or viewbook. Find out what your tour guide likes about the school community, dining hall, or traditions. Ask about her own experience at the school and how she's handled homesickness, the academic load, and time management.

In addition to your own questions, here are some other possible things to ask:

- What is it like living in a dorm full of kids your own age?
- What is there to do for fun on weekends?
- How did you cope with leaving your friends and family at home?
- What do most students do in their free time?
- What is your favorite campus tradition or event?
- How is the food, really?

Your tour guide is a student who lives this reality every day, and she wants to share her experiences with you. I told the tour guide at Pomfret that I was interested in squash, so she made an extra effort to show me the squash courts and answer my incessant stream of questions. We became friendly, and when I made the decision to attend Pomfret, I e-mailed her to let her know. In September, I was thrilled to find out that she was a prefect living on my hall. *(At Pomfret, prefects are student leaders who help faculty members lead each dorm unit.)* By asking educated questions and talking about your interests, you learn more about the spirit of the school, and you may even make a new friend!

After the campus tour, you will probably return to the admission building for your interview. This is often seen as the most nerve-wracking part of the campus visit. But don't sweat it (literally)—be excited! This is when you can show yourself off to the school. Demonstrate to your interviewer that you would be a great addition to the school community.

The interview is a time for honesty and reflection about why you want to make boarding school part of your education. Touch on moments from the tour and express what aspects of it you really liked. Hone in on what truly attracts you to the school. The interviewer's job is to make you feel comfortable. Interviewers talk to applicant after applicant, year after year—so don't be shy or afraid to converse with them! They want to find out what makes you tick.

Your interviewer may ask some of these questions:

- What is your favorite subject in school? What do you like about this subject?
- What books have you read recently outside of the classroom?
- What attracted you to this school?

- What current events are you interested in?
- What historical figure do you admire most?
- What are some of your passions and hobbies?

Be sure to answer all questions thoughtfully and thoroughly. One-word answers will not suffice!

At the end of the interview, there will be time for you to ask your interviewer questions. Always have some questions ready. Be sure to ask about matters that really spark your interest. This is also a great time to ask anything you may have forgotten during your tour. Here are some good questions:

- How is advising set up? Am I able to change out of my advisory group?
- Do students have a voice when it comes to making school decisions?
- How can I join a club?
- How many classes can I take per term, and what are your graduation requirements?

All schools are different, so remember to customize the question list to fit each school. This all goes back to doing your homework and preparing in advance.

Before you leave the school, your parents will meet for an interview as well. This is a time for them to ask all of their questions before the ride home. During this time, you may (politely) help yourself to the beverages, cookies, or snacks that most admission offices have set out for applicants. Most families are too nervous to eat or drink, so there should be plenty left for you. Relax, the hardest part is over!

When your parents are done with their interview, be sure to thank your interviewer as well as get his business card so that you can send an e-mail if you have any additional questions. Shake his hand and smile. You're one step closer to mastering campus visits.

When you arrive home, be sure to send a nice, handwritten thank-you to your interviewer and an e-mail to your tour guide. For your thank-you note, you may want to go to a local paper store and invest in some good-quality stationery. This adds a professional touch to the personal gesture. As I said, manners are appreciated and can only help you throughout the admission process. Be sure to follow up with any additional questions; these are helpful and confirm your interest in the school.

Later, sit down and take out a blank sheet of paper. At the top, write the name of the school. Make a two-column chart, with one of the sides being the positives of the school and the other side being the negatives. Then, fill in the columns based on your impressions from the visit. If you do this after every campus visit, the untouchable grandeur of all of these picture-perfect schools will become a clearer vision of realistic havens for you to spend your high school career. Make sure you go over these lists with your parents. Have a conversation and see if the school seems like a good fit. Keep these lists in a folder as the admission season goes on, and see if there are particular schools or trends that you like more than others. Come decision day in April, they could be very handy!

ABOUT SOPHIA CLARKE

Unlike almost every other American teenager, I never intended to live at home for high school. For as long as I can remember, boarding school seemed like a natural transition and the perfect choice for me. I toured and interviewed at fourteen schools around New England and finally found a home at Pomfret. Not only did I enjoy the search process, I also loved hearing about my friends' search experiences. At school, you can probably find me watching indie films or worrying about science labs.

CHAPTER 7
Revisit Days:
Finding the Right Fit

by Bennett Sherr
Phillips Academy Andover—Andover, MA—Class of 2017
Hometown: Princeton Junction, New Jersey

The day I understood what "fit" means in terms of choosing one's boarding school, I was standing with an admission officer outside Phillips Academy Andover's auditorium waiting for my not-so-punctual host student to arrive for Spring Visit Day. All of my fellow prep school "newcomers" had been successfully paired with their hosts and were off exploring the campus, the curriculum, and the cuisine du jour.

Suddenly, the silhouette of a young man appeared over the hill leading to the auditorium, and I watched him barreling toward us at breakneck speed.

"Whoa, Dustin! Hit the bag and slow down," the admission officer (and varsity baseball coach) said as he smiled broadly, choosing not to chastise my host for being tardy.

"Sorry, Coach!" Dustin beamed back as he hastily shook my hand and hustled me off at his own fast pace. And thus, I was shadowing—or rather, sprinting after—Dustin as he began his school day.

Whether it's called Spring Visit Day, revisit day, or something else, it's a chance for newly admitted students to experience life on campus before they make their final decision regarding which school they will choose to attend. For some, revisit day may be the first time they set foot on a particular boarding school's grounds. Others see this day as a second chance—after the on-campus interview and tour several months (and one acceptance letter) earlier—to get a taste of a school physically, intellectually, and socially. If a school does its revisit days well, which, in my opinion, means leaving them largely unscripted, you will leave with a gut feeling of your fit at that specific school.

The first stop Dustin and I needed to make on that spring morning was to the dining hall for breakfast, something else my host had put off until the last minute. After quickly grabbing a muffin from the buffet food service line, Dustin directed me to sit with a friend of his, Justin.

"Dude, what's with your pants?" he immediately asked Justin, who was sitting at a table in a pair of wild, polychromatic swim trunks.

"Yeah, this is all I have left. I guess I need to do laundry," Justin shrugged with a chuckle as he finished eating.

At that moment, I took a lightning bolt to my gut, exhaling my pre-revisit fears and welcoming a newfound, powerful sense of belonging. Dustin and Justin were my kind of people. They were not glossy brochure photographs with carefully groomed quote bubbles over their heads, or perpetually upbeat tour guides carefully instructed to remain, well, perpetually upbeat. Dustin and Justin were real students figuring it all out on what was, for them, a typical morning. Meeting Dustin and Justin during my revisit day was like watching wildlife during a safari as opposed to domesticated animals at the zoo. Observing students in their natural habitats can make or break the decision on which school to attend if you have a difficult choice to make.

A friend of mine, Aadhira, put her revisit day experience this way:

"I went to two revisits, one at a boarding school where I would be a day student and another at a boarding school hundreds of miles away where I would live on campus. I thought I knew the day student school well from inferences I had made by living near it for almost my whole life. The other school was my dream school, or so I thought based on its stats and application materials. I certainly put more time and effort into applying to this school, and my whole family was thrilled when I was accepted! Well, after a day of sitting in awkward silence around a classroom table with highly introverted students and eating cafeteria chicken nuggets with the consistency of bouncy balls, I was devastated to learn my dream school was not right for me. I simply couldn't picture myself there. On the other hand, the day student school that I thought of as merely a 'safety school' ended up surprising me even more! The sense of warmth and community I experienced there on campus was far greater than at the other school, and everyone seemed genuinely happy to be there. Revisits completely changed my mind, and I am tremendously grateful that I had the experiences at both schools before deciding where to go."

Aadhira's courage in embracing what she felt in her gut about the decision she had to make is admirable and was only possible because she attended revisits at both schools. She was able to cast aside some of the "application baggage" she was carrying around and really get a sense of how she would feel as a student at each school. Revisit days give you a clearer picture of a school, without the rosy fog that accompanies seeing a school before being admitted. It is different for every applicant, but some questions and concerns that a revisit can help you address include the following:

- I am supposed to be happy at this school because it is ranked #___ on a list of top schools, but I don't think I "feel the love." Is this the right school for me?

- My admission officer and I really hit it off well. Could he or she be the only reason I want to go to this school?

- The tour guide on my interview day was the only student I met, and I couldn't get a great idea of the student body as a whole from just one person. Will I like or dislike the majority of the students at this school?

- I think I might be choosing this school based on a specific program (athletic team, drama department, debate team, orchestra, etc.). Will I find other aspects of the school appealing as well?

- The school I have been admitted to employs the Harkness Method (or the Socratic Method, or another style) for its academic programs. Will I feel uncomfortable learning in this way, or will I find it easy to adapt?

- I looked at the school through rose-colored glasses on my interview visit, so everything about it seemed great. Now, I need to really figure out the pros and cons of the school. Or, I was so overwhelmed at my interview visit that I really didn't take it all in. I just have no idea what this school is really like. Or, my interview visit was so many months ago, and I looked at so many schools that I honestly don't remember what was so special about this particular school!

- My parents are convinced this is the school for me, but I'm not so sure. Or, I am convinced this is the school for me, but my parents aren't so sure!

While all of the other experiences you have along the road to matriculation are certainly important, your revisit day is one of the most significant and very last opportunities for doubts or affirmation before you need to commit to a school. Boarding schools will ask for your confirmation of their admission offer in writing and with a monetary deposit, usually about a week after the last revisit in mid-April. After revisits, you must accept or reject a school's offer. Choose wisely, because leaving home for a new "home away from home" is truly a life-changing decision.

SAMPLE REVISIT DAY

Each school takes a slightly different approach to its revisit days. But the following schedule is a general representation of what you can expect.

7:30–8:00 a.m.	Registration and refreshments
8:00–9:00 a.m.	Welcome and opening remarks by Dean of Admission and Head of School
8:45 a.m.	Students will leave parents and be paired with their student hosts and attend classes, following their hosts throughout the day. Students will be returned to parents by 3 p.m.
9:00–9:45 a.m.	Panel discussion: Academics Department Chairs and faculty members will discuss the school's academic program with parents.
10:00–10:35 a.m.	Sample classes for parents
10:45–11:30 a.m.	Panel discussion: Campus Life Dorm counselors, proctors, and medical directors will discuss the school's residential program with parents.
11:30 a.m.–1 p.m.	Lunch Students eat with their hosts in the student dining area; parents either eat in the student dining hall or at a luncheon hosted by the school.
1:15–2:45 p.m.	Dorm and campus tour for parents
By 3:00 p.m.	Students will be reunited with parents.
3:00–3:30 p.m.	Q & A session: Students and Parents Current students will share their personal experiences and answer questions.
3:30–3:45 p.m.	Closing remarks: Dean of Admission and Head of School
3:45 p.m.–??	On your own: Feel free to visit athletic practices or other parts of the campus (school store, art gallery, etc.).

MAKING THE MOST OF A REVISIT

It is important to remember that revisit days are very different from the visit and tour you had on campus during the interview process. I'll bet you were on your best behavior back then! In order for you to get the most out of a revisit, you must shelve your guarded interview-day persona and just be you. Remember, you received the invitation to the school's revisit day because you have already been admitted. Yes, they want you! Yes, you're in! Unless you do something profoundly moronic on your first full day on campus, they are not going to rescind their offer to have you join their fine institution.

As I said before, don't be afraid to ask questions. Gather as much information as you can from your host and the people he or she introduces you to. These are some basic questions you should feel free to ask:

- Is today representative of your typical day?
- What was the biggest challenge you faced as a new student?
- How would you characterize the academic rigor of the classes? What is your favorite class? Why?
- On average, how much time do you spend on homework per night?
- What is the social scene on campus? Is it easy to make friends?
- What is it like living in the dorm? What are the best dorms? Why?
- What do you do on weekends?
- How competitive are the sports teams? Do you find you can balance athletics and academics easily? If you are not an athlete, ask if the school has a basic athletic requirement per term (most do) and what level of competition you should expect.
- What clubs do you belong to? Do most students participate in extracurricular activities?
- Do you like the food? Is today's menu the norm? How often do you eat off-campus or order food to the dorm?
- What is the best part about attending this school?
- Are you happy here? If you had a second chance, would you pick this school again?
- Is there anything you would like to change about your school?

Be a detective! Look for evidence that confirms the reason(s) why you applied to this school. Take mental (or actual) notes on the school's environment. Here are a couple of things to look for and to ask yourself during your revisit day:

- Did you see evidence of all that the school promises in its brochures, websites, interview, and tour there?
- Do you feel that the school is genuine and supportive?
- Do you think that the school understands how to get *you* through high school and to *your* end goals, whatever those may be?
- Assess the relationships. Are students and faculty/admission officers building meaningful relationships with you and your family? Do you and your parents

feel that these people will still be engaged with your family after the enrollment process is over?

SUMMING UP THE REVISIT EXPERIENCE

William Leahy, Director of Admission at Phillips Academy Andover, leaves his prospective students and their families with this sage advice, "Never pick a school for 'next year.' Instead, pick it for your senior year. Remember that you are seeking a place that will challenge you, and if you pick a school that feels too comfortable before you even get there, it most likely won't end up being a big enough of a stretch for you by your senior year."

For me, my final revisit was at Phillips Academy Andover, a school that is extremely intimidating on paper, certainly to the point of being more than slightly uncomfortable. Even after getting the "golden ticket" acceptance letter, I was still not convinced that I truly belonged there. I carried application baggage in the form of fear that this school, by reputation, was academically cutthroat to the point of being impersonal and unwelcoming. I hadn't necessarily felt instant camaraderie with my tour guide six months prior, and I worried that I wouldn't fit in with what I feared the student population could be—cold, over-stressed robot geniuses cloaked in human flesh! To my relief, Dustin and Justin proved to be anything but robots. Instead, they were instant friends. Don't get me wrong; I have no doubt that Dustin and Justin are geniuses. One of them is even the author of a book you might be reading (cough, cough). But that lightning bolt that hit my gut when witnessing their friendly breakfast-time interaction was my indication that I'd found the right fit for me.

REVISIT BASICS

1. Your invitation to attend a revisit day will either arrive with your acceptance packet or shortly thereafter. Most schools will offer admitted students three or four dates to choose from. Select one day for your revisit, and RSVP appropriately. Having several revisit day options per school should allow you to make revisits at more than one school if you are fortunate enough to be considering multiple admission offers. Since many boarding schools follow similar admission cycles, the revisit days will most likely be at the end of March or beginning of April. The timing of the revisit days—a few weeks after acceptances are sent—is convenient, as it allows the shock of your acceptance to wear off and affords you ample time to make travel arrangements.

2. Parents and guardians are invited and strongly encouraged to attend your revisit day with you. At most schools there will be a special program for the adults, full of essential information about the school and campus life. The parent schedule will likely be separate from the admitted student schedule and include panel discussions with administrators, faculty members, house counselors, and current students. At some schools, parents may also have an opportunity to sit in on a few classes to experience the academics firsthand.

3. It is important to abide by the individual school's dress code during your revisit. If the school does not follow a particular dress code, feel free to dress casually but smartly. You do not need to wear your best interview outfit to a school where the students will be in jeans and t-shirts. In order to feel comfortable at the school, you will want to blend in with the students on campus as much as possible. Of course, this also means wearing a jacket and tie at schools where that is the expected class dress uniform.

4. Arrive on time for your revisit, and stick to the schedule.

5. Observe, participate, and engage. Raise your hand, open your mouth, and ask or answer questions! Instructional practices vary from school to school; use your time in the classroom to get a feel for the school's academic culture and whether you feel you could be successful there.

6. Make connections. Aside from meeting your host and his or her friends, meet other students and fellow revisit-day participants. After all, those current and prospective students could end up being your classmates, dormmates, roommates, and lifelong alumni friends. When choosing your school, you also choose the people you will be surrounding yourself with for the next four years. Meet as many as you can before you make your decision!

7. Ask questions. If you ever wanted to know anything about dorm life, academics, athletics, campus culture, or anything else pertaining to the school, revisit day is the time to ask! Current students will generally give you their honest views and opinions; revisit day is a much more authentic environment than scripted admission events. In addition, your host will probably give you his or her contact information either before or after your revisit. Feel free to use it if you think of a follow-up question after you have left campus.

ABOUT BENNETT SHERR

My recent acceptance to five of the country's most selective boarding schools was not preordained fate—in fact, it shocked everyone! Despite a legacy of many generations of public school alumni, I arrived at the decision to apply to boarding schools after spending a month in a French-immersion program on the campus of a Swiss boarding school. Hooked on the boarding student life but unable to convince my parents that I should live abroad full-time, I returned to pursue boarding schools in the United States. I researched, interviewed, toured, tested, applied, and worried throughout my eighth-grade year. Luckily, my middle school résumé as an honors student, two-year varsity captain of the wrestling team, two-term member of the student council, and all-around nice guy won over each admission office. I credit my revisit experiences with convincing me that Phillips Academy Andover was the perfect boarding school for me.

CHAPTER 8
The Packing List: What to Bring to Boarding School

by Alicia Schultz
Hebron Academy—Hebron, Maine—Class of 2012
Hometown: Palos Verdes, California

I once saw a post on the Internet (most of my stories start that way) that said, "The most unrealistic thing about *Harry Potter* is that they only bring one trunk of stuff to school." This statement touches on one of the most challenging tasks I faced throughout my high school years. It's possible that I could write two chapters on this subject: what to bring to boarding school if you live close enough to fill up your parent's car, and what to bring if TSA restrictions mandate that you fit everything in a couple of suitcases (and maybe bring a little more when you return to school after Thanksgiving or Christmas break). But for brevity's sake, I will confine this list to the necessities, which (hopefully) will comply with TSA regulations.

SCHOOL STUFF

- Your school will generally offer an opportunity to go shopping for school supplies before classes start, so you might not want to waste luggage space for these things. That said, if you have a favorite style of binder, pencil, or something else, feel free to bring it in case that particular type can't be found at a store near your school.

BED STUFF

- Sheets, pillows, etc. Most beds will be extra-long twin size (twin XL), but you should check with your school to make sure. These items can also be bought once you've made the journey, but you'll have more options if you get your bedding ahead of time.

- Mattress covers, pads, and toppers. A lot of school mattresses have been around for many years. Get a mattress cover and pad to give yourself a fresh surface to sleep on, along with possible protection against dust mites and allergens. You may also consider bringing a foam mattress topper if you feel that you need added cushioning.

- Bed risers (if your school allows them). These are more useful than you might think. Storage space is going to be tight, so it helps to give yourself some extra space under your bed.

COMPUTER STUFF

- A laptop is definitely recommended. You're going to want versatility and portability, so a desktop is not the best option. On the other hand, tablets like the iPad are too small to handle all the functions you need.

- A printer is optional. Some schools have community printers in every dorm or study space, while others afford you limited access to outside printers. Make sure you know what your school provides and recommends.

DORM STUFF

- Shampoo, body wash, towels, and other shower essentials are definitely required. You'll also want a shower caddy to carry and store these supplies. One thing that works for me is to have two shower caddies, one smaller than the other. I keep the larger one in my room, and whenever I bring the smaller one back from the shower, I place it inside the other to avoid messy drips and spills. You may be wondering why you can't just leave your caddy in the bathroom. Well, you can, if you don't mind people "borrowing" your products.

- Space savers are really helpful. Hanging shoe organizers, for example, can be used for holding many other things in their convenient pockets. Like I said before, maximize your storage space.

- Laundry detergent, stain sticks, rolls of quarters, and a laundry bag or basket are also important, even if you sign up for a laundry service. You never know when you will need to run a few items on your own from time to time.
- A power strip is essential. So few outlets, so many chargers.
- Don't forget about speakers. I especially recommend the kind that runs on batteries, so you can blare your music in the bathroom while you shower (if your dorm's rules permit).

DECORATIONS

- Make sure you learn and follow your dorm's rules about putting up decorations. Some will forbid pins in the walls; others will forbid pins in the walls but not care about that rule whatsoever (I'm looking at you, Hebron Academy!). If your school happens to actually enforce this rule, getting wall putty or wall-safe tape is advisable. Also, look for over-the-door hooks and mirrors to avoid making unnecessary holes in your walls, as your school might charge you for room damages when you move out.
- Many school regulations are based on potential fire hazards. It's a good idea not to buy things like beanbag chairs or dangling lights until you fully understand your dorm's rules.
- Once you are aware of the regulations, go for it! You'll be living here about nine months of the year, so you're going to want to feel at home when you step into your room. Make sure to pack family photos and your favorite posters, as well as any other memorabilia or trinkets that will make your room feel like home.
- If you have a roommate, though, keep your things to your side unless you've worked out some other arrangement.

FOOD AND MEDS

- Most schools should allow nonperishable food. You might want to get a lock box as food theft may be fairly prevalent.
- Don't get a mini-fridge unless you have the school's permission. Don't plan on storing too many perishable food items unless you know you have access to a communal dorm refrigerator or are allowed to have a small one in your room.

- Some schools will allow you to keep your own prescriptions and simple pain meds in your room, but this is another thing you need to check. At my school, pain meds are one of those "technically not allowed but not an enforced rule" items, but prescription medications have to be given to the dorm parents to pass out to you at a regular time each day.

CLOTHES

- Again, this is somewhat school-specific. For example, if you go to a school with a strict dress code or uniform, you won't want to bring as much in terms of what you now consider regular school clothes, such as jeans and hoodies. No matter how strict your dress code, however, it is a given that you'll need some nice clothing. Ladies, make sure you have a few nice dresses and skirts; guys will need to have a suit and some nice ties and blazers. Add to or subtract from this wardrobe based on the needs of your school.

- You will have down time, of course, so don't leave out casual clothing completely.

- If your school is in New England, like many U.S. boarding schools are, be prepared for inclement weather. I am a California girl who went to a Maine boarding school, and let me just say, I was not prepared. My mentality rapidly changed from "I don't like coats, bring on the cold!" to "I am an icicle! Save me, fleece jackets!" So be sure to consider your location when planning your wardrobe. New England calls for fleece, scarves, boots, gloves, and other forms of protection from the snow, cold, and rain.

- Don't forget workout wear and sports equipment. A lot of boarding schools require students to be on a sports team in lieu of (or in addition to) physical education. You will probably be given an opportunity to acquire or rent the necessary equipment for your sport before the season starts, but if you already know what sport you're going to play, don't forget to bring your own equipment.

- This may be mainly for the ladies, but guys should pay attention as well. Try to maintain some sense of modesty in your sleepwear. You might have dorm parents of both sexes, and they don't want to see . . . that. My friends and I will always (fondly?) remember the awkwardness of one of our male dorm parents, who always knocked an excessive amount of times when he came to check in with us.

Him: [KNOCK KNOCK KNOCK] It's Mr. Flynn! Can I come in? [KNOCK]

Us: Yes, come in!

Him: Are you sure?

Us: Yes!

Him: [pause] I'm coming in! [long pause]

Us: [open door and stare at him exasperatedly]

As ridiculous as these encounters always were, he was sparing both himself and us the undue embarrassment of being caught off guard, and it was sweet. So treat your dorm parents with a little respect, and try to keep your loungewear more modest than just underwear.

RANDOM STUFF

- Think about getting a Netflix or Hulu membership. For better or for worse, much of your free time in your dorm will involve sitting with your friends on a bed, watching stupid movies or episodes of *Law & Order*.
- Bring some cool snacks you can only get in your hometown/country. There's no better way to make friends than with free food!
- Be sure to stock up on napkins, disposable bowls, and plastic utensils. How else are you going to eat that microwaveable mac and cheese?
- Febreze® or whatever other air freshener you like is a necessity. Sometimes, dorms can get a little smellier than desired.
- Consider signing up for Amazon Prime, Zappos, or another online shopping with shipping service. You won't have regular access to shopping centers, so it is important to have a way to buy things in a pinch.
- Don't forget to bring important paperwork and emergency numbers.

I hesitantly mention the following:
- A bicycle. Some campuses are bigger than others, and a bicycle may be practical at a sprawling school or if your dorm is located on the edge of campus. Or maybe you just like to ride bikes! Feel free to bring one if it's possible, but don't go to school under the impression that this is something you'll need, because it's not.

- A personal Wifi hotspot, which is offered by several phone companies. I feel slightly uncomfortable with this recommendation because some boarding schools shut off their Internet access at a specific time on weeknights (it was 11 p.m. for me). You'll need to decide if you're willing to spend the money and, more importantly, if you're willing take the risk if your school does not approve of a personal Wifi hotspot.

So there you have it, a list of boarding school necessities from a student's perspective. I have left out some of the obvious things, like chargers for your electronics and hangers for your clothes, but you should now have a pretty comprehensive list of the important items for boarding school life. In addition to this list, you should look over your school-supplied and school-specific packing list provided with your housing and orientation materials. Happy packing!

ABOUT ALICIA SCHULTZ

I didn't consider boarding school until halfway through my freshman year in high school, when I learned I had to move to Louisiana. I wasn't thrilled with that prospect, so I started looking at boarding schools as an alternative. Ten applications and several months later, the acceptances started arriving. As a competitive skater, I chose Hebron Academy because of its high-quality ice-skating rink. Because life is funny that way, I didn't even end up using the rink much at all. But I never regretted my choice. At Hebron, I was involved with soccer, tennis, musical theater tech, the Gay-Straight Alliance, and the school newspaper, and I was inducted into our Cum Laude Society my junior year. To this day, I remain incredibly grateful for the time I spent at Hebron. I learned a lot and met the most amazing people. The boarding school experience was a fantastically positive one for me, and I hope my contribution to this book will help other students find their right school. I now attend college at the University of St. Andrews.

CHAPTER 9
Leaving Home: Saying Goodbye to Friends and Family

by Sloane Wilten
The Hill School—Pottstown, Pennsylvania—Class of 2016
Hometown: Bethlehem, Pennsylvania

W hen people think of high school, they usually envision friendship and drama and the smell of sweat leaking from a gymnasium, nestled between loud metal lockers and worn linoleum floors. What doesn't cross their minds is an air of tradition wafting through venerable brick-and-ivy edifices on a campus where students learn *and* live. People don't often think of teenagers dealing with the ups and downs of high school without living at home.

When I found out I was moving from my beloved and friendly Southern state to a Northern one where I believed that people would sneer at my Southern smiles, I was immediately distraught. I was midway through eighth grade, and my friends and I thought that we were going to go to high school together. We were all surprised and intrigued when I got accepted to a boarding school that I had applied to because of its proximity to my new hometown. The concept of a live-on-campus school was foreign to us (not many people we knew applied to or attended boarding school). I was going to be one of those rare few, and I did not really want to go. I wanted to stay with my friends and go to school with them. I didn't want to move again, but obviously it wasn't my decision to make. Going-away parties were thrown, tears were shed, luck was wished, and goodbyes were said as often and as loosely as hellos. And in early September, I found myself stepping onto The Hill School's beautiful campus and up to the key-card-only-accessible door of my dormitory, the place that I was now expected to call home.

As my parents drove away and I was left in a room with a girl I had only known through Facebook for the past few weeks, a wave of unsettling doubt washed over me. That month was full of firsts, and I made new friends while I struggled to keep my old ones. My friends from back home tirelessly struggled to make our long-distance friendship work. They texted, called, e-mailed, and Skyped me, but I found myself overwhelmed with orientation activities and places to explore. I did my best to respond when I could, but whenever I said, "I'm busy, but can we talk later?" I started to notice sighs of frustration and slight shifts in tones of voices at the other end of the line. My friends were becoming aggravated with me, and I didn't know what I was supposed to do. They wanted to hear about everything that was going on, but I quickly became busy and grew tired of trying to explain my daily routines to them. While I thought that whatever I was saying would only make sense if my friends had been there, they started to drift away from me, annoyed that I couldn't keep filling them in on everything. Who knew it would be this hard to keep a friendship alive?

I had been calling my parents almost routinely at this time, and I would highly recommend that you do this as well. (I have friends who didn't get in touch with their parents very often in the early months of the school year, and they all wound up wishing they did.) For some reason, it was easier to tell my parents things than it was to tell my friends back home. My parents supported me through every little thing I complained about. When I ranted about my friends from home, they listened. When pangs of nostalgia prompted me to beg that they take my sisters and me back down South for Christmas break, they obliged.

At the beginning of the holiday break, it was strange to be with my family, without my roommate a few feet away as well as four other girls on my hall, and it was even stranger to see my friends. But to be honest, seeing my friends was only awkward for a minute, and then it was like I had never left. We hung out at the mall and went to a movie as though I didn't live 800 miles away from all of them. I think that if you have the right friends, it won't matter how many miles away you live or what school you attend. The only thing that matters is that you remain a good friend when the time comes to be a friend in person.

Now that my mind was at ease about my old friends from home, the main challenge of adjusting to boarding school life was the fact that I missed living with my family. Some days, I would be hanging out with my friends and feeling so lucky to be a part of the school, but other days I just wanted to go back home. I wish I had known at that time that pretty much everyone else was going through the same thing. Homework was stressful, exams were looming, and I just wanted summer vacation to arrive. Along with that, my stomach was killing me, and I couldn't figure out why.

My parents offered several times to let me switch schools if I thought living away from home was too hard. Every time, I considered the offer and then declined. When I thought about it, I realized that I loved being part of something greater. At my school, I had freedom, I had fun, and I had another family. My boarding school had become my larger, more diverse, but equally lovable extended family. I had 600 brothers and sisters now. And my parents still made me feel comfortable with my real family. If living away from home has taught me one thing so far, it's that I take my parents for granted much too often.

At this point, though, I was still trying to figure out why my stomach wasn't feeling well. Why was I so stressed lately? Was it homesickness? I ruled that out because my homesickness from the very beginning of the year didn't feel like this at all. Was it the academic rigor catching up to me? I didn't think that was a possibility, because I'd been in challenging schools my entire life. Is it me? Is there something wrong with me? When I called my mom and asked her the same question, she laughed, and I knew instantly that I needed to stop analyzing so much. I realized that the feeling in my stomach was just unnecessary worry! Instead of making myself sick with anxiety, I needed to just be grateful for the amazing opportunity I was given, grab all of my chances by the horns, and make something amazing of myself. I mean, that is what boarding school is all about, right? Unfortunately, I discovered this at the very end of the year. Seniors were reminiscing, and students were buzzing with sudden pre-summer energy.

Graduation rolled around, and I watched the seniors cry together. They walked down the hill leading to the old hockey rink, clad in white dresses or khakis and standard graduation blazers. They received their diplomas, said their farewells, and jumped into the pond, as per post-graduation custom. Dirty pond water and tears dripped down their shirts as the traditional "Welcome Alumni" sign was hoisted. And, as I watched my two prefects (who are the best of friends) hug each other and cry, I knew that I was happy to be here. I knew that I was lucky, because I wanted what they had: I wanted to be so close with somebody that we would be like siblings. And when I said goodbye to my roommate and the rest of the girls on my hall, *I* started to get emotional. The funny thing was, I would be seeing them all again in three months (and every day for the next three school years).

Watching the seniors jump into the pond to christen their graduation, carrying out century-old traditions, building unbreakable bonds, and growing to love my extended family—this is an abbreviated list of the things that make my heart swell with pride for my school. You may think that I'm crazy to adore a school, of all things, this much. And maybe I am crazy. All I know is that I wouldn't want to go to high school anywhere that I felt any less of a clichéd, heart-warming, opportunity-filled sense of affection. I swear I am not being paid by the school to write this; I now honestly love riding the roller-coaster lifestyle of boarding school, and I wouldn't change a thing. No wait, that's wrong. If I had to change one thing, I would go back in time and tell my pre-orientation self something.

And here's what I would say: "It's going to be okay."

That's it. I wish I had known those five little words before the start of the school year. I would have appreciated the beginning a whole lot more and spared myself a whole year of uncertainty. Now I only have three years left of my boarding school experience. I am most definitely not saying that it isn't a tough and trying journey, because it is. Boarding school could very well be the biggest odyssey of your life, and I have one last piece of advice:

There will be rough waves. There will be storms. And the only light you have to guide you is the fact that the ocean you're in can be the most beautiful one in the world. But the ocean will only show you its beauty if you have patience and let the waves settle. So wait out every storm, stop to fix your broken masts, and gather perspective on the world around you. I promise it will all be worth it.

HELPFUL TIPS WHEN YOU ARE FEELING BLUE

- I learned too late that pretty much everyone else was going through the exact same thing I was. They might put on a brave face, but trust me—everyone gets to a point when he or she starts to miss home.

- I wish I had known not to feel guilty about being too busy to keep in touch with my old friends. Now I know that this is so unbelievably normal and that breaks and vacations are the perfect times to reconnect with friends from home.

- Consider stopping by the campus student health center. In addition to a nurse and/or doctor, every school has a psychological services or support center where students can speak to counselors. They are there for a reason. Often you'll feel better when someone whose job it is to listen to you does just that.

- I have found that my parents are very compassionate and helpful, and it was incredibly valuable to have them as my invisible, but very strong, backbone. If you have a close relationship with your parents and siblings, keep in touch with them.

- Go to extra academic support sessions. That is an easy and useful way to build deeper bonds and connections with teachers. You'll find that your instructors are trustworthy adults who usually live on campus and are there to support you through thick and thin.

- If you do get ill (stomach flu, common cold, fever, skin rash, and so on), GO TO THE HEALTH CENTER! Unfortunately, your mom is not close by with her chicken soup and hugs and kisses, so seek help on campus. But, also, be sure to have some essential items on hand in your dorm room for emergencies: Tylenol® or Advil®, throat lozenges, vitamin C, anti-itch cream, and (one of my personal lifesavers) a tummy ache/stomach flu kit that includes saltine crackers, a few cans of ginger ale, a few bottles of sealed Gatorade®, and even Tums® or antacids. Put all of these in a sealed box under your bed for emergencies.

- Whenever I hit a rough patch, I make a list of the pros and cons of boarding school before acting on my feelings. I always ask myself these questions, too:

  —Do the pros outweigh the cons, or is it the other way around?

  —Am I really alone at this school?

  —Do I have a strong support system here?

  —Do I feel at home here, or is it all still extremely alien?

  —Do I think that this experience will all be worth it for me? (Ask yourself this question very honestly, without the influence of what anyone else says.)

My Strategies for Managing Stressful Situations:

- Take a deep breath. Or three. Go to a calm place (either in your mind or an actual place where you can be alone) and think about whatever is causing you so much trouble. Attempt to realize that the whole ordeal may seem insignificant within a year, or maybe even a day.

- Remember "IGBOK." (It's going to be O.K.)

- Start a journal. I know it sounds cliché, but I've found that venting on paper helps. Once you read each entry over, you might realize how overly dramatic you're being. Sometimes, it even makes you laugh, which helps. I've been told that if you can learn to laugh at yourself, it's a good thing.

- Ignore stereotypes. In high school people reinvent themselves often, sometimes on a daily basis. Forgive and forget—and that includes yourself. Don't be your own harshest critic. Give yourself (and others) a break sometimes.

- Talk it out with someone. For me, there were lots of "someones": my parents, my friends, and my counselors.

ABOUT SLOANE WILTEN

I recently moved from Nashville, Tennessee, to Bethlehem, Pennsylvania—just one in a series of big moves and changes in my life. I was born and raised in London before we moved to America several years ago (sadly, I don't have an accent anymore, but my British roommate does!). I'm used to change; I've moved around a lot and attended many schools. For my family, allowing me to attend boarding school was a difficult decision, but I honestly could not be happier. At The Hill School, I participate in the musical theater department (some tech and some acting), and I am also on the varsity golf team. I think that boarding school is a fantastic opportunity, and I applaud you for choosing to attend, being accepted to, or even considering it.

CHAPTER 10
Orientation: The Basics—
Getting Acclimated

by Olivia Paige
The Taft School—Watertown, Connecticut—Class of 2015
Hometown: Watertown, Connecticut

For any student, the word "orientation" often prompts mixed emotions. Orientation can be good or bad, fun or not so fun, easy or embarrassing, but it's something that every new student has to go through at some point. I still look back and laugh at my first day at Taft as a new sophomore, and reminisce about the hilariously awkward orientation encounters. Orientation was a chance for me to meet other new students who—even though I refused to admit it at the time—were probably feeling as embarrassed as I was. Now that I've been through that awkward orientation stage and have had time to reflect on it, I'd like to help you make the most of your orientation and your first day, week, and year at boarding school. Here's a list of things I either did, wished I did, or hope you'll do at the start of your first year.

DON'T Be Shy on Move-in Day
On move-in day my first year, I was pretty nervous about what was yet to come. If you asked me then and there what I regretted most about orientation, I would have said just showing up. But now, I'd say it was not getting out there and meeting as many people as possible. Move-in day is the easiest day to meet new people, and you don't even have to worry about asking, "What's your name again?" because everyone is asking the same thing. It's a day to familiarize yourself with your campus and get to know other students in your class and dorm. At my school, it's a tradition for the varsity football team to help all the girls move into their dorms (can you predict the awkwardness?). Just my luck, my roommate's boyfriend was the one who

helped me move in. It took four trips to the car to get all of my things, and I was scared that my roommate and her friends were all judging me. Then, I cracked a joke about how my parents decided to just move my whole room, and it was all laughs for the remainder of my move-in. Now that football player is one of my best friends, and that roommate still pokes fun at me in a lighthearted way.

DO Introduce Yourself to Other New Students

Chances are, they're feeling the same way you are. Introducing yourself to other new students not only makes you appear social and confident, but it helps you connect with others who are in the same situation as you. One of the first girls I met on my first day is still one of my close friends, partly because we bonded as we went through everything together during orientation. She was always there when we didn't know where to sit in the dining hall, needed to find a class, or didn't want to walk to a school event alone. We still laugh at the uncomfortable ice breakers, silly mistakes, and awkward interactions during our first couple of weeks. Having a buddy or two during orientation can certainly make things easier as you get adjusted.

DO Introduce Yourself to Returning Students

Likewise, introducing yourself to students who have been at the school for a while can also be extremely beneficial. They probably know a lot of people, where every class and building is, and valuable tidbits of information about campus life. At Taft, we have Old Girls/Boys, upperclassmen who act as your older brother or sister and help you get through the first few weeks of school and sometimes even become one of your favorite people at the school. Mine had been in touch with me since a few weeks before school started and answered any questions I had about moving in. Throughout orientation, she showed me where all of my classes were and helped me navigate Taft. She not only calmed my nerves and eased my first-day jitters, but she remained someone to turn to for advice throughout the rest of the year.

Whether your school has a similar buddy program or if you just have monitors/ prefects in your dorm, I cannot stress enough the importance of getting to know returning students. They can help you get settled, teach you traditions or special things at your school, show you where to sit in the dining hall, and help you avoid so many potentially embarrassing new-kid moves.

DO Make the Most Out of Orientation

As reluctant as you might be to admit it initially, there is a reason for the madness of orientation. Don't be that person who sits out of orientation activities because you think they aren't fun or because they're embarrassing. Some of my best memories from the beginning of school are from those ridiculous icebreakers up in the sweaty, crowded gym. Orientation isn't the place to act like you know everything or to think that something is stupid or pointless; it's a chance to make a complete fool of yourself, meet new people, and experience things at your new school. I promise that you'll regret being unenthusiastic about those orientation activities because they are easy opportunities to make new friends and get to know your classmates.

DO Find Where Your Classes Are Before the First Day of School

No one, and I repeat no one, wants to be that new kid asking the senior for directions to your first class when you're already running late on your first day of school. I know from experience that you will never live that one down. Almost every new student is walking around the day before classes trying to figure out where his or her classes are, and there is no reason why you shouldn't, too. Grab your roommate or a few friends and make it an adventure—then, by the first day of classes you'll be familiar with the layout of your school, and you'll probably meet a couple new people along the way!

DO Get to Know Everyone in Your Dorm

There's nothing more boring than a night spent just sitting in your room. As most boarders can tell you, some of the weirdest, craziest, and most fun and memorable moments in your boarding school career will happen in your dorm. (Day students, this doesn't exclude you. Feel free to stop by a friend's dorm on a weekend for some outrageousness and bonding.) However, if you don't get to know your dormmates, these experiences are much less likely to occur. You're living with these people, so you might as well get to know them, right? The kids in your dorm, along with your dorm parents and prefects/monitors, gradually become one big family. These students will become not just your friends and classmates, but your surrogate brothers and sisters. You'll be surrounded by them constantly, so there's really no reason not to get to know them. In particular, reach out to those who share your interests, are in your classes, or play the same sports as you, and you'll feel much more comfortable when you see them in the future.

DO Reach Out to Adults on Campus

They aren't out to get you, I promise! Dorm faculty, teachers, coaches, and advisors are there to look out for you and guide you in the right direction if you need it. They're there to drive you to Starbucks to get some hot chocolate and de-stress before exams, to help you reevaluate your study skills when not every test is going as well as you would like, and to support you both in the classroom and beyond. Personally, I consider my advisor to be like my second mom, and she's always there for me. You might not realize it at first, but the student/faculty dynamic at a boarding school is so much different from at a day school. You don't just see your teachers for class—they'll also be coaching you, monitoring your study hall, having dinner with you, and chaperoning weekend events. It's in your best interest to get to know them and your dorm parents sooner rather than later, because they are some of your best on-campus resources. Whether you're homesick and need some comfort, or just need a trip to the local CVS pharmacy, faculty will be there for you, and it's crucial that you reach out to them when you need it.

DO Sign Up for Clubs, Activities, and Sports

This one is pretty self-explanatory. It's the easiest way to meet people who share your interests. Don't be afraid to sign up for tons of clubs or activities, because it's much easier to stop later on than it is to join halfway through the semester. Through clubs, activities, and sports, you'll meet a lot of new people with a varying range of skill levels and experience in something that interests you. Plus, they give you a nice break from schoolwork and a way to hang out with friends while doing something productive with your time in the afternoons and weekends.

DON'T Be Afraid to Be Yourself

Last but not least, don't be afraid to be yourself! Boarding school is a great opportunity to start with a clean slate in a completely new and different environment, and you will only be able to get the most out of it if you don't hold back. Boarding school is a place for you to grow as a student, build your character, and experience things you may have never experienced before. You only have a few years, and it's so important to give them your all. Try new things, build upon something you already love to do, start a club, challenge yourself with different sports or rigorous courses, but most importantly, just be yourself. That's what the boarding school experience is all about, and it all starts at orientation!

ABOUT OLIVIA PAIGE

I was born in Greenwich, Connecticut, and raised in Fairfield, Connecticut, and I'm one of the preppiest girls you'll ever meet. I chose to go to boarding school because my previous school felt too small, and after starting as a sophomore, I'm happy I made that decision. I'm a boarder at The Taft School and am co-editor of *The Annual*, our yearbook. I also row on our crew team, am a proud member of the junior varsity hockey team, and do almost all of the photography and some of the videography on Taft's website. My dorm room is covered in monograms, photos with friends, and posters and photos from concerts I've been to.

CHAPTER 11
Dorm Living: Roommates, Laundry, Communal Bathrooms, and More

by Emilee Bae
The Hotchkiss School—Lakeville, Connecticut—Class of 2014
Hometown: Los Angeles, California

Possibly the scariest thing about boarding school is the actual boarding part. Moving into a dorm can be intimidating, exciting, and surprising all at once. Some schools have vertical housing, meaning that all four grade levels are represented in each dormitory facility. Some have split housing, with lowerclassmen in some dorms and upperclassmen in others. A few schools even have freshmen-only dorms and separate dorms for non-freshmen. At some schools, day students get rooms and roommates, and at others, day students aren't part of dorm life at all. No matter what the housing system is at your boarding school, there are a few general things to take into account.

ROOMMATES

A lot of schools like to give freshmen roommates so that new students will have a quick friend and someone with whom to figure out the swing of things. Over the summer, the housing office will most likely send you your roommate's name and contact information, so you should be able to get in touch before move-in day. It's a good idea to reach out to your roommate, whether over the phone, through e-mail, or (most likely) on Facebook. Your school probably had you complete a questionnaire to help gauge your personality (e.g., if you like to stay up late, if you are messy, if you listen to music while you do homework, and so on). Your roommate probably had very similar answers to yours, so you likely won't be complete opposites. Some people shy away from talking to their roommate from before they arrive all the way through the first few days at school. You, however, should do quite the opposite. Talk to your roommate about anything: the sports you're interested in, decor for your room (couches, refrigerators, area rugs, posters, etc.), classes you might have in common, tastes in music, and favorite movies and TV shows (you two will probably spend quite a bit of downtime on Netflix and Hulu together).

Many people worry that they won't get along with their roommates or that they won't have anything in common. While that can occasionally happen, most unnecessary discomfort can be avoided if you start off the year by being open-minded and ready to compromise. Try to be as courteous as possible, especially within the first few days when you aren't yet really comfortable with each other. Offer your roommate her choice of the beds and desks if you don't have a strong preference. Ask your roommate if she wants to go to dinner with you on the first night so you'll both know at least one person in the crazy and hectic dining hall. If you want to listen to music while you unpack, ask your roommate if that's okay, and then ask for song suggestions. Offer to turn the lights out so she doesn't have to get out of bed, even if you're farther from the switch. Always ask before you borrow anything from your roommate, and offer to lend your things in return.

In many ways, boarding school makes students a lot more independent, but living with a roommate can dial back some of those freedoms, especially if you're used to having a room of your own. If your roommate wants to go to sleep, it's more courteous to finish your work in the common room, in the hallway, or by only using a desk lamp rather than the overhead light. If you're polite and relaxed, your roommate will be too, and soon, you'll find a system that works for both of you.

That being said, sometimes there are tough-to-solve issues between roommates. As you get to know your roommate, you will learn how best to approach her. Some people are good with discussions and are open to hearing what you have to say. Others can be a little defensive and won't see why something that bothers you is a problem. Don't be afraid to ask for advice from your advisor, your dorm parents, or even friends who have dealt with a similar issue or know your roommate. It's always a little awkward to confront someone, but once you take a deep breath and say what's on your mind, it's a relief to have the issues out on the table. Chances are, your roommate may have been trying to find a way to bring up the same issue with you, or she had no idea that this was bothering you and will quickly make an effort to change.

If you have a problem with your roommate's habits or mannerisms, think about whether it's something you can tolerate, or if it's something you need to address before the tension comes to a boiling point. Confronting your roommate about letting her side of the room get a little messy is different from confronting your roommate about always having guests over when you're trying to sleep. Some things aren't worth nagging them about and other things definitely are. Just stop and think about how much something *really* affects you before you call it to attention.

On the flipside, if your roommate has a problem and comes to you about it, try not to get offended! Hear her out and take a step back. Imagine that it's your friend being approached by her roommate about this issue; what would you advise your friend to do or say? Try to be as calm and understanding as possible. Don't let yourself get pushed around, but remember that you have to share this space at least until the end of the year, and conflict is the last thing you'll want to deal with on top of a rigorous academic load.

You and your roommate will develop a system for how things work around your mini-home. You'll learn each other's sleeping habits, favorite snacks, morning routines—all of it! In some ways, it's a little creepy. You'll know more about each other than you bargained for. Even if you do know each other's habits, try to be as helpful as possible. There are chores to be shared, and you'll soon figure out who is more inclined to do what. For instance, I always take out the trash and vacuum the carpet, while my roommate is in charge of wiping everything down with disinfectant wipes (make sure to get those door handles and light switches!) and shaking out the rugs. It's an unspoken agreement that just developed out of habit, but it works for both of us.

LAUNDRY

Most schools have laundry services available so that the students don't have to worry about washing their own clothes and linens. While these services can sometimes be expensive, they are convenient and helpful. Signing up for a laundry service for your first year doesn't have to be a life-or-death decision. If the drop-off/pick-up system turns out to be too complicated or you realize you don't trust anyone else with your clothes, you can just take your name off the list the next year.

Sometimes, laundry services accidentally mix up or lose pieces of clothing. It's unfortunate, but it happens. Most students who use a laundry service choose to send off only their everyday apparel, like work-out clothes, socks, undergarments, linens, towels, and casual attire. Students can sometimes pay for a higher level of service to wash more delicate pieces, like dry-clean only sweaters and formal attire, or they pack them up and bring them home to be cleaned during breaks and long weekends.

Many students, however, elect to do their own laundry. This process eats into your time, but it is certainly more affordable. Most schools have laundry machines in all the dorms, and a few let students utilize Laundromats in town. If you're going to do your own laundry, your parents will probably get a letter about setting up a school debit card so you can pay for your loads. While these cards are convenient and easy, the systems tend to break a lot. You should always keep a stash of quarters in your room to pay for the machines in case the cards aren't working. There's nothing worse than going down to the laundry room to switch your clothes from the washing machine to the dryer and finding out that the card reader just went out of service. Then you're running around campus like a lunatic looking for $1.25 in quarters to put your clothes in the dryer before they mildew. You'd be surprised by how hard it is to find five quarters at a boarding school.

If you've never done your own laundry before, don't worry. Boarding schools know that complicated machines with multiple dials and buttons make even less sense to students than the college selection process. Basically, you put detergent into the machine, add your clothes, pay, and press either WHITES or COLORS. Occasionally you'll come all the way down to the laundry room, when your clothes were supposed to be done, and find out that five minutes into the wash cycle your load became "unbalanced." All that means is that your clothes wound up on one side of the agitator, and you just have to even it out again. It's a pain, but it's by no means a disaster. Once your clothes are done in the washer, just switch them over to a dryer. Pop in a dryer sheet if you want, pay, and then hit the desired level of heat—low, medium, or high—whatever setting makes sense for what you're drying. When it's done, and hopefully everything is totally dry, try to fold your clothes as soon as you possibly can. Congrats, you've done it!

Ten Tips and Common Courtesies

1. Write your name on your detergent and dryer sheets and keep them in your room. When you go down to do your laundry, just toss them in your bag on top of your clothes and bring them back to your room when you're done. It's no fun to buy a bottle of detergent and then, when you go to use it, find that it's only half full. And when people steal your detergent, they almost always get the sides all nasty and gunky. Even though it's just soap, no one wants to touch that!

2. Furthermore, don't be that kid who steals other people's detergent and dryer sheets. It's always awkward when you try to subtly borrow detergent from someone who's left her bottle in the laundry room and then she walks in and sees you pouring her detergent for your load of clothes. There's really no way

to come back from that. If you ran out and forgot to buy more detergent at the store, go ask a friend if you can borrow some of hers, and offer to lend her some if she ever runs out. If you forget to buy more again, go ask a different friend.

3. Don't let your laundry sit and fester in the washer for a few millennia before going to get it. If you let your soggy clothes sit in the washer, they can start to mildew and get smelly. That's just gross. Another hazard of leaving your wet clothes in the washing machine is that some impatient person will eventually come and take your clothes out and just leave them on a table or atop another machine. You don't know what she may have dropped on the floor and then just thrown back onto the pile. So much for clean clothes! Sometimes, if it's a really crowded laundry day (Sundays and any time many parents and/or grandparents are on campus), people run out of places to put someone else's soggy laundry, and you may find your wet clothes on the floor with the lint bunnies. Then you'll get grossed out and end up doing the load all over again.

4. Don't leave your clothes in the dryer forever either. If you leave your clothes in the dryer, they'll cool (obviously). But when they cool, they will keep whatever scrunched up form they were in when they were warm. Then you'll either walk around looking like a smashed accordion, or you'll have to iron your clothes—and that's a whole different art that most boarding school students are not ready for. If you get your clothes hot out of the dryer, you can smooth and fold them while they're still warm, so they won't get all wrinkly.

5. Clean out that little lint thing in the dryers. I'm sure that this apparatus has a proper name, but no one knows it. There's a little wire mesh tray where all the fuzz collects in the dryers, and it doesn't matter what color your clothes are, the lint is always gray. Try not to think about it too much. Just pop out the little sheet and take it over to the trashcan. It might seem sort of gross, but it's really just loose thread fibers that have all been through the wash, so it's as clean as the clothes you're about to walk around in. You might initially want to just bang the sheet against the trashcan until the lint falls off, but you'll immediately regret it when all the dust flies up into your face. Just peel the fuzz off and you're done. I always try to get it all off in one go, but the clump generally breaks. Check to make sure the tray is empty when you put your clothes in, and if you have time, try to clean it after your load is done. It's just a nice thing to do for the person after you.

6. If you have a ton of laundry to do, don't take up all the laundry machines! Multiple loads at once are too much to handle, anyway. Put one load in, and

then when you move the first batch to the dryer, put the next one into the washer. That way, if someone else only has one load to do, she is not stuck waiting for you to finish all four of your loads. Also, bring some homework down to the laundry room so that you can keep feeding your clothes into the machines efficiently.

7. Don't wait until you have no socks or underwear left to do your laundry. I've been in this situation more than once (always seems to be midterms or finals week), and it's so *stressful!* You should probably do your laundry once a week (you'll be surprised by how much you have to wash). At least every two weeks or so, change your sheets and wash the ones you had on as well. Don't forget to toss in your towels whenever you do laundry, too.

8. Don't try to cram all your laundry into one load to save money. I do this all the time, and it never works out. I don't really wear much white, so all of my laundry goes into the "colors" load. If I've been busy and I haven't done my laundry in a week and a half, the load is a really awkward size. In this case, it's better to do two smaller loads than one monster load. If you do a monster load, your clothes won't really spin in the washer. Thus, they won't really get clean; they'll just sit there in soapy water. Then, when you put your clothes in the dryer, they won't dry completely either. At the end of the cycle, they'll still be damp, and you'll have to pay for another cycle.

9. If you need something ironed but don't have time or know how to iron, here's a simple trick. Take the item and put it on a hanger. Grab a garment bag or trash bag, and cover the item with the zipper slightly open or a tiny slit cut in the trash bag. Hang this contraption in the bathroom and take a nice steamy shower (or make your friend go take a shower if you can't spare the time). The steam will release the wrinkles without you having to risk scorch marks from the iron.

10. Go to Target and buy every pack of Hanes socks on the rack. You will probably want to get a few basic colors like white, black, and gray. I don't know why, but the washing-machines-eating-socks thing is alive and well at boarding school. You'll always end a laundry load with one sock in search of its mate. Trust me, your supply will dwindle fairly rapidly, and it will be awful. If you have a ton of colorful socks, you'll probably lose their pairs, and eventually you'll stop caring, so you'll walk around with one blue sock and one green sock all the time. If you're cool with that, that's fine, but it bothers me to no end.

COMMUNAL BATHROOMS

Communal bathrooms will be a huge adjustment for most students. But after about two days and one shower in each stall, you'll be totally settled. Right before lights out (if your school enforces it, especially for underclassmen), the bathroom will be like an airport terminal during the holidays. There are simply not enough sinks for all your dormmates to brush their teeth and wash their faces without dripping water everywhere. Try to brush your teeth about 15 minutes before you're supposed to be in your room, because several things can go wrong if you wait until the last minute:

- Someone is going to laugh and spit toothpaste onto the back of your head when you're bent over the sink. Or her toothpaste/mouthwash will get too spicy for her. Either way, it happens, and it sucks.

- People will have water dripping off their faces, and they'll have to maneuver through everyone for a paper towel. They will dribble their face-water on you, and—even if it's just water—something about it is gross and weird.

- Too many people will be crowded around the sinks trying to brush their teeth. If you're short like I am, this means you will be elbowed in the eye. If you wear contact lenses like I do, this means that your contact lens will be shoved out of your eye by this motion and it will hurt. Then you'll be trying to shove your way to the sink to spit out your spicy toothpaste while crying out of only one eye like a deranged Cyclops. And then you'll have to get down on your hands and knees to find your contact lens on the nasty bathroom floor while trying not to get run over by the stampede. It's happened to me, and it could happen to you. Just brush your teeth early.

There are a few things about sharing a bathroom with other people that might be no-brainers, but I'll just add them anyway. First, you might want shower shoes. As you get more comfortable in the dorm, you'll probably ditch the rubber flip-flops. But for the first few days, you'll want the shoes as a backup, just in case the shower really grosses you out. When you use the sink, try to wipe down the countertop really quickly. I don't know why, but dorm sinks are like waterparks. There are always splashes on the counter, and it's annoying for no real reason. It's no big deal; just try to wipe it down if you've made an ocean.

I'm not going to lie, I sing in the shower all the time. Usually if I'm alone, I'll just start singing because I get bored. However, once the water's on, it's hard to hear if anyone else starts a shower. There's nothing more frightening than when you're just doing your thing, and some voice two showers over joins in at the chorus. If you're going to join in, you might want to say something first, like, "I love that song!" or,

"You have a pretty voice! Who are you?" Chances are that if you started showering at different times, you'll get out at different times and may never learn who that mysterious person was who joined you for the chorus of "Call Me Maybe." It will plague you forever. If you're going to sing in the shower, make sure it's not at a bad time. Don't sing during study hall. It'll be awkward if someone has to come into the bathroom to tell you to be quiet so other people can study. Don't sing late at night, and definitely don't sing early in the morning. Other than that, I guess it's fair game.

DORM PARENTS AND PROCTORS

Dorm parents and proctors, or whatever your school calls them, are your parents away from home. You're not replacing your real parents; your dorm parents are just a more immediate source of advice and authority. Your dorm parents and proctors are great resources, and you should never be afraid to go to them for help. Proctors (also known as prefects at some schools) are usually upperclassmen who live in the dorms to enforce lights out and study hall, organize dorm events, and help their "proctees" in many ways. Since the proctors are also students, a lot of people feel more comfortable going to them for social and academic advice because they've more recently been in similar situations. Both dorm parents and proctors are great assets to every dorm. Even if they might seem intimidating at first, remember that they really want to get to know you. Don't be afraid to start a conversation with them, especially at the beginning of the year. Even if you don't get super close with the faculty member on your floor, there will most likely be at least one dorm parent in the whole dorm that you'll get along with. Likewise, it doesn't matter if your favorite proctor isn't on your floor, as long as you find one somewhere in your dorm that you can rely on.

FROM A DORM TO A HOME

At first, living in a dorm can be awkward and scary, but once you settle in, it will become a home. You'll befriend neighbors you never would have been friends with otherwise, and they'll help you find your place in your new environment. Dorms, especially floors or halls, can become tight-knit families. Sometimes, dorms can get crazy or loud (teenagers running around wreaking havoc occasionally get a little out of hand), but it's an experience that's beyond worth it. Within the dorm, you'll form bonds that you just can't form any other way, and that will stay with you forever. Even if dorm life sounds daunting at first, you'll adjust in no time, and you'll always have those dorm parents or proctors to help you through any rough patches along the way. Living in a boarding school dorm is a fun and fulfilling experience that has given me many lasting memories.

ABOUT EMILEE BAE

I decided I wanted to go to boarding school when I was in fifth grade, after reading a book in which the main characters attended a fictional boarding school in Vermont. The situation in the book seemed like so much fun that I knew that I wanted a similar experience. At Hotchkiss, I play field hockey, and I'm involved in the Arts Club and magazine (*INKredible*), Knitting Club (this could be embarrassing), LiNK (Liberty in North Korea), Classics Club (as in ancient Latin and Greek—I'm a nerd), and Outing Club (an outdoor adventure/ hiking club). In my free time, I love reading, horseback riding, hiking, listening to music, and being with my friends and family.

CHAPTER 12
Adults Are Important:
Teachers, Mentors, and More

by Lillian Costello
Maine School of Science and Mathematics
Limestone, Maine—Class of 2015
Hometown: Milo, Maine

Someone once told me, "It's not what you know; it's who you know." And although I don't always agree with this maxim, I do believe that it's a valuable piece of advice for someone at a boarding school. In most cases, students entering boarding schools know few, if any, classmates at the school, and even fewer faculty or staff members. As you probably know, it's important to build relationships with other students, because they're obviously the ones with whom you're going to attend school, graduate, and go off into the world. Yet ultimately, it is the faculty members who are going to help you through school, supervise your graduation, and prepare you for wherever your dreams may take you. So even though friends are a huge part of the boarding school experience, adults sometimes play an even larger role.

GETTING TO KNOW YOUR TEACHERS

Now I don't know about you, but I chose to go to a boarding school for academic reasons. As someone who is passionate about learning, the first thing that I would recommend all new students do—especially academically inclined ones—is to build relationships with teachers. Even if you don't plan to dabble in academia after graduation, and instead want to be a professional athlete, for example, your relationships with teachers are still very important. You may not believe me now, but when you suddenly realize that your science teacher has a friend or relative somehow linked to the NFL, you'll be wishing you had listened to me. Every teacher has connections, whether these connections are in academics, athletics, business, or anywhere else. But the only way you can tap into these connections is to build a good relationship with your teachers. So now you may be thinking, "Well, that's all fine and good, but how on earth do I befriend my teachers?" And the answer to that is fairly simple.

First of all, you have to make yourself stand out (in a good way) to your teachers. This can be somewhat tricky, depending on which boarding school you attend. For me, I only have 100 other students in my grade, whereas some boarding schools might have double or triple that. Don't worry if you have a lot of classmates, though, because standing out isn't really all that difficult. It's just a matter of going the extra mile, or putting in some additional effort. For instance, make sure to go to a teacher's extra help sessions or office hours if you're struggling in the class. Even if you aren't having trouble, those meeting times are still very helpful. And try to stay after class, if possible, to ask questions of the teacher. Initially, these questions should probably be related to the course's subject matter, but as you build a relationship with the teacher, you can gradually start to (appropriately) ask more personal, philosophical, or imaginative questions. While you are doing this, don't forget to show up to class on time and prepared for the day's activities.

Secondly, always remember to inform your teachers of your goals, if you have any. When I say goals, I mean academic, personal, career, or any other goals that you may have that will help the teacher get to know you. For instance, every teacher I have knows that I want to become an astronaut. Although not directly pertinent to everyday school life, this helps my teachers get to know me better and remember me. You want your teachers to know you as well as you know them, since it's a two-way relationship that you're trying to build.

Moreover, always make sure to be friendly to your teachers. Even if you've failed a test or are doing poorly in a class, there's no reason to hate a teacher, or to think that your teacher hates you. Teachers are there to help you succeed in their subject—that's why they teach. They don't expect you to be a straight-A student; they just want you to invest effort and care into their class. So don't get down on a teacher because he's given you a bad grade on your math test. Chances are, he's not doing it because he dislikes you. Be friendly—kindness always goes a long way!

Of course, there's not really one right way to cultivate relationships with teachers. The steps that I've just laid out are good guidelines for befriending your teachers, but there are always other ways to do things. Just remember, teachers are a valuable asset to you in your high school career (and at any other school you attend, for that matter). Building good relationships is always to your benefit, and a lot of times, you'll find that your teachers are genuinely interesting, nice people.

GETTING TO KNOW YOUR RI

The next group of people that you should have a good relationship with is the residential staff. Although all boarding schools are different in this respect, in general, you're going to have an adult who's in charge of looking after a group of students during the night hours. For our purposes, I'm going to refer to this person as the residential instructor, or RI for short. Basically, your RI is there to make sure you're following the rules of the dorms, like any lights-out policies or dorm clean-up duties. However, the RI is also there to make you feel more at home. If you're ever having any problems—academic, personal, or otherwise—you can talk to your RI. That's part of an RI's job. So how do you get to know your RI? That's my next topic.

Getting to know your RI is just like getting to know any other person. You'll probably see your RI a few times a day, and when you do, be sure to smile and say hello. Of course, you're also going to want to try to have more regular conversations with her. Regardless of whether those conversations are about problems that you're having or last night's sports game, it's still important to have them. Now you might be asking yourself, "Why should I go out of my way to do this?" Well, it's important to have someone in the dorms that you're comfortable talking to. This is especially helpful if you have to deal with a family crisis while you're at school. These issues are hard enough to go through when you're at home, but when you're far away from your family, there're even harder. Trust me—I learned this after having some family trouble of my own. Initially I was not at all prepared to talk to my RI about it. But luckily, my roommate got my RI for me, and I told her what was happening. This ordeal would have been a lot easier for me if I had already built a solid relationship with her. But I didn't have the opportunity to read this chapter (or a helpful book like this!), so I didn't think it was necessary to bond with my RI. You, on the other hand, have just been forewarned. Don't make the same mistake I did.

CHOOSING YOUR MENTOR

Now the last thing to do, after you've cultivated all of these relationships, is to find a mentor. Your mentor is an adult on campus with whom you can openly and comfortably talk. Eventually, you might even consider your mentor a good friend. This mentor is someone who can get you through to the next day and keep a smile on your face when you're feeling down in the dumps. So how should you choose a mentor? It's not something you do hastily. It took me until spring of my freshman year to find mine, and for some people it takes longer than that. Regardless, you should definitely find one at some point in your high school career.

First of all, remember that being a mentor is an unofficial position. This person has a real job, too, so don't expect your mentor to spend all of his time on you. That said, good mentors will dedicate as much time as they can to helping you.

When it comes to finding a mentor, you should think about the teachers and staff members whom you like and respect. If you are seeking a career in a field that is specific to one of your teachers, you may want to consider him as a mentor. However, this isn't always necessary. Really, the defining characteristic that you want to look for in a mentor is someone you can trust and in whom you can confide. That said, you don't just force the duty of mentor upon anyone you wish; you have to let it come naturally. It would be weird to just walk into some random teacher's classroom and say, "Hey, will you give me helpful advice and spend time with me until I graduate from this school?" That's not a good strategy. You have to bond with a faculty member at a natural pace. Then, if you find yourself spending more time in a particular teacher's office and you are doing this not only because you want extra help but because you genuinely want to spend time with the teacher, you have found your mentor.

For me, the person I would come to call my mentor was my academic advisor during my freshman year. He also taught a class to all new freshmen, which included me. Although I didn't fully realize it then, I was starting to spend a lot of time in his room, whether it was for the German Board Games Club or just to talk. Then, early in the second semester, when I was dealing with a death in my family (a trying experience that I hadn't been through before) he reached out to me. Once that happened, I realized that I felt comfortable talking with him, and that he had some really good advice. That's when I knew I had found my mentor. Since then, I have visited his classroom almost every day.

Here are some things to remember when seeking a mentor:

- A mentor can be any adult on campus: teacher, residential instructor, janitor, you name it!
- Make sure that you genuinely like this person.
- Be certain this adult knows exactly what you hope to accomplish, in both the short- and long-term future.
- Remember that this person will probably be your mentor for the remainder of your time at school, so choose wisely!
- Don't force the choice; it will come naturally.
- Technically, you can have more than one mentor. It's important to build a meaningful relationship with your mentor, however, so don't have too many.

- Always remember to thank this person for being there for you and giving you helpful advice. Faculty members aren't required to be mentors, so don't take them for granted.

There you have it. Teachers can help get you to where you want to be, residential staff can help you through personal issues, and your mentor can do all of those things and more! But don't take my word for it—go out and discover it firsthand!

ABOUT LILLIAN "LIL" COSTELLO

I chose boarding school because I wasn't being challenged academically at my local school. So I ventured up to the coldest part of Maine to go to high school. At Maine School of Science and Mathematics (MSSM), I am the Astronomy Club president, a Boffer president (a fitness club that teaches medieval fighting skills and weapon building), the assistant head of the Admission Ambassadors, and the secretary for the Student Senate. I can always be seen wearing a hat and trying my best to become an astronaut.

CHAPTER 13
Time Management: Avoiding All-Nighters

by Sarah Cho
Kent School—Kent, Connecticut—Class of 2014
Hometown: Plainview, New York

If there's one thing almost all students learn from their boarding school experience, it's time management. According to the boarding school alumni I've talked to, figuring out how to manage time on your own before college is a real blessing. And although almost every boarding school graduate heads to college with a good understanding of time management, this chapter will give you some tips and tricks, so you won't have to learn these skills the hard, painful way.

When I say the hard, painful way, I mean when you realize a bit too late that if you had managed your time properly you would not have had to pull an all-nighter, scramble to learn material minutes before an exam, and exhaust your brain so that it does not operate properly during the test. Believe me, you do not want this to happen. And now I hear you asking, "So how do I avoid this awful fate?"

Well, it all begins at the beginning: in class. First and foremost, be organized. Have a different, designated notebook, binder, and/or folder for each class. Legibly write the date on everything you get and every new sheet of notes. Next, give your undivided attention to your teacher and classmates. Listen carefully to what the teacher has to say, and take good notes. By good notes, I don't mean take down everything that comes out of the teacher's mouth. Rather, you should:

- Take down crucial points of the topic.
- Use bullet point or outline form. Complete sentences aren't necessary.

- Use abbreviations, like "/" for "or," ">" for "more than," and "↑" for "increase." Over time, you will probably find yourself developing your own shorthand, which is a good thing and will allow you to take better, more in-depth notes.

One thing that makes boarding school special is its widespread use of discussion-based classes (some schools call this the Harkness Method) where students are taught by engaging in discussion rather than solely through their teacher's lectures. Teachers provide important information as a basis for conversation, and students build off of it. Don't be afraid to participate in the discussion; your opinion and knowledge will be valued by the class. Active engagement in these types of classes helps your brain do a better job of processing the information in your notes. You will be able to learn a lot more by participating, which will help you when it comes time to study.

Also, when your teachers announce assignments and upcoming evaluations, make sure to write down those dates. Don't think this is necessary? You'll find out that you're wrong when there are so many different due dates, exam dates, club meetings, and sports practice times to keep track of that your head is spinning. Here are the five steps you need to take to ensure that you remember everything important and keep up with your busy life as a prep school student.

1. **Get an agenda or planner.** Whether your agenda is an actual book, an app on your phone, or a calendar on your computer, make sure you have a place to take down the assignments for each day so there won't be a paper you forgot to submit or a quiz that caught you by surprise.

2. **Next to each homework assignment, write an approximation of how long you think the assignment will take.** By the end of the first week of school (which is also the length of time teachers tend to be forgiving about forgotten or incomplete assignments), you should have an idea of how long a particular type of assignment should take. Thomas Hunt, my advisor and sophomore English teacher, notes, "If you determine that you have 3 hours of homework, you'll obviously need to find 3 hours of time to do it. Where do you find that time? Before dinner? At a study hall? During a free period?" Mr. Hunt also suggests that the difficulty of the subject should influence the order in which the homework is done. He advises, "Homework that uses up the most mental energy should be done first, while your mind is fresh."

3. **Put together a daily schedule that also indicates blocks of time when you're going to do homework, go to and come back from sports, and eat dinner.** Why are schedules so important? One of the tips I picked up in a new student seminar is that schedules give you a better sense of control. For example, during swim season, it's especially important for me to have a schedule. The girls share the same pool with the boys and divers. This means

that swim practice is at a different time every day (sometimes even during study hall). Having a schedule has been crucial in helping me figure out when to do homework while dealing with a demanding athletics schedule.

4. **Do not wait until Sunday to start weekend homework.** Even if your school has a few classes on Saturdays, do some homework for other subjects on Friday nights. Finish some work on Saturday as well, so that you don't panic Sunday night.

5. **But don't be overly strict with the schedule either; be realistic and allow yourself some leeway so that it doesn't fall apart. Give yourself ample time to rest.** It's important to take a breather outside in the fresh air (I know, fresh air can be a foreign concept at times), eat that yummy snack you've been saving, or talk with some friends. You need to go easy on your precious brain. My house counselor likes to remind us to set a "stop-work" time and stop working then. For me, even during the notoriously tough junior year, my "stop-work" time was midnight. At that point, I would stop my work, do my nightly routine, and jump into bed. If you take advantage of every free block in your day and structure your time in a manner intended to allow you to complete everything by your "stop-work" time, you will almost always finish by the "stop-work" time.

I know, a lot of you might think it's impossible to get to sleep by midnight if you have multiple tests and quizzes the next day. The key is studying ahead of time. Your teachers will usually give a week's notice of test dates and a few days' notice for quizzes (or else students tend to revolt in fury). The weekend before the day of multiple quizzes and tests, get a head start. Here are a few tips.

TIPS

- Begin organizing your notes, handouts, index cards, chapter outlines from online, and so on.
- Split the material into subtopics.
- Spread the studying over a few days, studying a couple of subtopics per day.
- Figure out which subtopics you need to concentrate on the most and make sure you are able to review these in great depth <u>before</u> the night before the test. That way, if you don't understand a part of the material, you have enough time to ask your teacher for help. By studying ahead of time, you won't need to stay up extremely late the night before your exams.

Another misconception is that it's impossible to avoid an all-nighter when there's an essay due the next day. You should spread out writing an essay or completing a project over multiple days, just as you would do when studying for tests and quizzes. Don't plan to save essays and projects for the last minute—they are designed to be done over a long period of time.

For essays, split the process into three parts:

1. Brainstorm and find textual evidence to support your thesis.
2. Write a rough draft of your essay.
3. Edit the rough draft and create a final draft. (It is better to have fresh eyes when you edit, as opposed to editing right after you finish writing.)

Projects follow a similar pattern:

1. Do your brainstorming and research.
2. Gather materials for your project.
3. Write a rough draft.
4. Edit the rough draft and create a final draft.

This way, you won't have to stay up all night before a project is due. Break up what you need to do over a considerable period of time, and pencil it into your schedule.

If you follow all these tips throughout the term, you will be a lot more prepared for the final exam than you think. Generally, I start studying for the final the weekend before the last week of the term. Figure out which classes are hardest for you, and start studying for those classes earlier. An advantage to this is that you can find your teachers with time to spare if any questions arise during review.

That said, my advice up until now is useless if you don't learn to concentrate—it is a crucial element of time management. My house counselor is absolutely correct when he says, "When you're reading something, you should not be looking at your phone or mentally cataloging what else you have to do that day. When you're writing, you should not be clicking over to something else on your computer." So, to make sure you're truly concentrating when you're doing schoolwork, try the following:

1. **Keep your phone on silent and put it far from your reach.** During a break from studying, reward yourself by checking your ever-so-important texts.

2. **Stay away from social media during homework time.** If you don't have the best self-control over checking Facebook every 5 minutes, install a website blocker. I've blocked all social media and video hosting websites between the

hours of 4 and 11:59 p.m. That way, I won't be tempted by TV shows or the Tumblr dashboard, but I still have Internet access for schoolwork. Some think my method is extreme, but it's surprising how much time you can waste on social media websites. By switching back and forth between Facebook and your assignment, you will be wasting time by having to constantly readjust your flow of thoughts. One of my instructors, Mrs. Booth, said, "A boarding school student's schedule is hectic, so it's important to take advantage of every little chunk of time. Even just 10 wasted minutes can hinder you in the long run." Keep in mind that the 10 minutes you spend on Facebook here and there eventually add up.

3. **Find a distraction-free environment to do your studying.** I cannot stay in my room with my roommate if I'm trying to get work done; we are extremely counterproductive when we are together. Instead, I head to the library and take over a cubicle. The library is normally where students can silently and seriously complete their work, so it's a great distraction-free zone.

In all honesty, I slept a good amount for a junior, sometimes even more than friends whose classes weren't so rigorous. If I hadn't actually used these tips I've given to you, I'm pretty sure I would have quickly sunk in the sea of schoolwork, despair, and many sleepless nights. I definitely slept more than I did at times during my sophomore year because I've now learned to manage my time more efficiently. I can say with confidence that these tips have worked well for me during my two years at boarding school, and I hope you can learn from them, too. Best of luck!

ABOUT SARAH CHO

I attended a public high school where most of my classes had more than 25 students. I couldn't help but compare the education provided at my old school to the one I received at the Summer School at Phillips Exeter Academy in 2008. Not only was the learning process absolutely amazing, but the experience was life-changing. So I decided I wanted to go to boarding school. I applied to be a repeat sophomore—a decision that wasn't made lightly. Ultimately, I concluded that an extra year at a great institution wouldn't be the worst thing in the world and that I didn't want to risk my junior-year grades by switching to a new school. I enrolled in Kent School, one of the best decisions I've ever made in my life. At Kent, I'm a tour guide, peer counselor, staff writer for *Kent News*, co-founder of the Sandy Hook Promise Club, and co-captain of the varsity girls swim team. I also volunteer and tutor at Kent's education centers and am a member of many other clubs. Outside of school, I volunteer at hospitals, teach Korean School classes, intern at the Children's Museum of the Arts, and am an art editor of *Boardspace* magazine, an online blog and literary magazine for the boarding school community.

CHAPTER 14
Papers and Essays: Write 'Em Right!

by Rena Patel
The Webb Schools—Claremont, California—Class of 2015
Hometown: Upland, California

M any people have come up to me and asked, "Hey, Rena, how do you write such amazing papers?"

And I usually say, "Dude, it just happens."

Actually no one really asks me that, and writing an essay, unfortunately, doesn't just happen. That said, I do know how to write a paper, and with this step-by-step guide and some helpful advice from yours truly, you, too, can write an amazing essay if you sprinkle in a little effort, knowledge, and your own brilliance.

WHAT TO EXPECT FROM YOUR FIRST BOARDING SCHOOL ESSAYS

The first couple of times you write and turn in an essay at boarding school, you will probably be disappointed. Transitioning from a middle school English classroom to the lofty expectations of any high school is challenging, and it's even harder at a boarding school, where the bar is generally set much higher. It doesn't matter if you came from a public school or a private school. Your first essay grade will likely be lower than what you're used to. I got a C on my first-ever essay assignment at The Webb Schools, and I had even taken Honors English in eighth grade. But don't despair, for higher expectations mean that you have more to work for and more to achieve. And once you meet those expectations, you're a step closer to surpassing them and becoming a better writer than you were before. So work hard, because there is a payoff! Here's how to do the best you can on your essays at boarding school.

Step One: Know Your Topic

When your teacher assigns a paper, he or she has usually already given you some basic information about the topic. Sometimes, teachers have a specific topic they would like you to write about. Other times, they will give you a general idea or broad theme, and they want you to figure out where to go with it. In both of these situations, research is essential. Your limited stash of information from your class notes won't always be enough, so it is up to you to broaden your knowledge base on your topic to craft a good essay.

So, to quote Hermione Granger from *Harry Potter*, "Go to the library!" Search for books on the topic you're researching in history; find an article expressing a theme analyzing a text you're discussing in English. I know, flipping through the pages of a thick volume seems like a trivial and arduous task, especially when we have such beautiful resources like the Internet to help make researching faster, but teachers like to know that you've put time and effort into your essays. They also want to make sure you know how to navigate through a lot of information to seek out exactly what you need. Also, the more information you have from different sources, the better your essay will be. My sophomore history teacher always told my class to search for as many pertinent sources as possible. That way, we would definitely have enough information to write a strong essay.

Break Time: A Crash-Course on the Five-Paragraph Essay and Thesis Statement

The thesis statement is an ideal way to start a five-paragraph essay. When you have three points in a thesis statement (one point for each body paragraph), you are on the right track to writing a five-paragraph essay. It is incredibly important to know about five-paragraph essays, as a lot of teachers assign them. This type of essay is an excellent way to organize your thoughts into precise paragraphs with a set introduction, three body paragraphs, and a conclusion. Five-paragraph essays aren't as threatening as they sound. As long as you don't wait until the night before to write the essay, the process is actually quite simple. But because of the five-paragraph essay's set structure, it leaves less room to really individualize your essay.

Now, not every essay needs to be a five-paragraph essay. In my high school career, I've written three-paragraph essays, fifteen-page papers, and everything in between. However, five-paragraph essay or not, the thesis statement sets the stage for the body of your essay. A strong thesis statement indicates a strong essay.

Step Two: The Introduction

The introduction is arguably the most important part of the entire essay. Simply put, it sets the tone for the rest of your essay. If you think about it in terms of a movie, the introduction is the "Morgan Freeman voiceover"—it lets you know what you should expect without giving away the entire movie. Your first few sentences will be your hook, which is an idea that immediately grabs the reader's attention. The hook can be a simile, a quote, a humorous anecdote (like the one I used to start this essay), or any other intriguing thought. If you were to write a paper on Renaissance fashion and how clothing was different for each social class, for instance, you could use an informational hook by writing, "In Leonardo da Vinci's famous painting, the *Mona Lisa,* the subject is pictured without eyebrows. Interestingly, in the time of the Italian Renaissance, it was a fashion statement for members of the upper class to shave them off." While this hook isn't being used as evidence to directly support an argument, it does introduce the subject of Italian Renaissance fashion in an engaging way.

After the hook, you proceed to the body of your introductory paragraph, where you establish the general idea of your essay. So, if we were to continue our fictitious essay on Renaissance fashion, we would write something like, "The era's rich artistry and expression gave way to new, avant-garde styles of clothing and fashion."

From the body, we move on to the last and most vital part of the entire introductory paragraph: the thesis statement. The thesis statement provides the layout of your entire essay. If we put it into movie terms, it's the critical moment where the protagonist realizes what he or she has to do. For example, in *Spiderman*, when Peter Parker realizes that a spider bite gave him unique abilities, everyone watching the movie knows he is going to end up becoming a superhero. Viewers thus want to find out how he puts these powers to use. Similarly, a thesis statement is that moment of realization where your audience has a general understanding of your essay's structure and storyline. Your readers don't know all the details, but the argument has been laid out, which is enough to make them want to know more. An example of a thesis statement for our paper would be, "Even though the Italian Renaissance was a time of new thought and prosperity, there was still a huge gap between elite and poor Italian citizens, evidenced by differences in wardrobe, hair, and cosmetics." This thesis statement specifies exactly what the essay will be about. After reading this thesis statement, the reader knows that the essay is about the differences in appearance of the upper and lower classes in Renaissance Italy.

The following is an example of our bare-bones introductory paragraph. When crafting your own, feel free to use a couple more sentences to fully transition from your hook to your thesis statement.

In Leonardo da Vinci's famous painting, the *Mona Lisa,* the subject is pictured without eyebrows. Interestingly, in the time of the Italian Renaissance, it was a fashion statement for members of the upper class to shave them off. The era's rich artistry and expression gave way to new, avant-garde styles of clothing and fashion. Even though the Italian Renaissance was a time of new thought and prosperity, there was still a huge gap between elite and poor Italian citizens, evidenced by differences in wardrobe, hair, and cosmetics.

Step Three: The Body

Now that we have our introductory paragraph, it's time to move forward to the body. This is, as you may have guessed, the largest part of the essay. The body is where you convey hard facts as well as your own opinion to your readers. The body can have as many paragraphs as you need to fully address your topic, unless you have been specifically told to write a certain number of paragraphs (like the five-paragraph essay).

TIP

Try using the **M.E.A.L.** system to easily outline a body paragraph's structure.

M: This is the **main** topic of your paragraph. It should be introduced in the first sentence of your body paragraph.

E: This stands for **example.** After the main topic is introduced, you should have an example that supports your main topic.

A: Next step is **analysis.** This is where you analyze why your point is valid and prove that your topic contributes to the overarching subject of the essay.

L: This is the **link.** It's the concluding sentence of your paragraph that links you either to your next topic (starting M.E.A.L. all over again) or to your conclusion.

The body is where you mold useful bits of information into coherent ideas for your readers to process. This is where all of that researching and your abundance of knowledge on your topic will come in handy!

You will definitely not use every single piece of information you've collected through your laborious researching, but you should have more than enough to create a good-sized body that fully conveys your thoughts to readers.

Step Four: The Conclusion

For me, the conclusion is the hardest part of the entire essay. When I first learned how to write a conclusion, my instructions were, "Just restate the thesis statement, but don't use the same words. Also, make sure you identify everything you wrote in your body paragraphs, but don't reiterate it in a boring manner. And don't forget to find an interesting way to tie everything together and end the essay." Needless to say, I was a little confused.

To simplify, a conclusion should be a brief and accurate overview with a final thought. In a conclusion, you want to be as straightforward as possible while making sure that all of your main points are accurately articulated to the reader one last time. The final segment of your conclusion should be a succinct thought on your subject. Your final thought could be anything from emphasizing the idea in your essay to relating it to another topic.

In our Renaissance essay, a shortened example of a conclusion could look something like this:

> The Renaissance's influx of new ideas influenced the wardrobe of each class. The quality and supplies used to create distinct clothing for the different classes reflected the society of the era. Even today, clothing, hairstyles, and cosmetics are used to distinguish a person in society, and they remain ways to analyze people based on their appearances.

The conclusion brings together the topics that were discussed in the essay, and it takes it a step further by relating the topic to another.

Step Five: Drafts and Proofreading

I know what you're thinking. You already have to write one essay, so you don't want to do it two or three more times. I completely agree with you, but taking the time to write more than one draft of your essays really helps. The process of putting your ideas down on paper and building upon those ideas with each draft is extremely valuable for you as a writer. Not every essay has to have a rough draft, but it is a great way to catch your mistakes and fine-tune your essay. The only time I had to turn in a rough draft for a grade was in my sophomore year's Honors Modern World History class. My rough draft earned a score of 18 out of 20. My final draft, which I turned in a week later after going through my teacher's comments and edits, received full points. Bottom line: your essay *will* get better with every draft.

Proofreading is another practice that writers should adhere to religiously. Proofreading is the action of revising your draft. As a writer, I've realized that you can look at your own writing in two ways. The first approach is, "Oh my gosh. This is terrible. Did I actually write that?" The second is, "I don't see anything wrong with this, so it must be good." Both of these are reasons why you should not be the only person to proofread your work. Thus, you should find a friend (or teacher if that is allowed) to proofread your essay. Different eyes see things that your eyes missed. I make my friends read through most of my work, and they're pretty good about it, too. In fact, I've had two of them review this essay (Thanks, guys!). Also, most boarding schools have office hours or writing centers where you can ask teachers and peers for help. This is the absolute best time to let your teacher have a look at your essay to give you feedback. Your teacher can spot things that your friends may have missed. Asking your friends for help and seeking help during office hours or at a writing center are great ways to get feedback on your work.

WARNING: PLAGIARISM

Plagiarism is when someone takes the work of another and falsely represents it as original. It is considered intellectual theft to plagiarize. This is something you should NEVER do. And I'm even breaking a rule of sophisticated writing by writing "never" in all caps to prove this point. So please, do not plagiarize. Do not even think about doing it. You will suffer major consequences if you plagiarize someone else's work. At boarding school, you will probably get a zero on the assignment, have to appear before a court of your peers or faculty, be suspended, or worse. On the bright side, avoiding plagiarism is easy. In research essays, when you are using someone else's work to help convey your idea, just be sure to cite your source. Whatever citation format your teacher has you use (MLA, *Chicago Manual of Style*, Turabian, etc.) is your friend. Learn it, know it, cite it. There are thousands of formatting guides for citations online. You can even use a website like Noodlebib that helps format your citations for you. And if you need extra assistance, go to your teacher—he or she will probably be more than happy to walk you through everything you need to know about citing your sources.

The most important thing you should know about writing an essay is that you are the creator. The words flowing onto the page are your thoughts and only yours. In truth, there is no exact way to write the perfect essay, because there is no such thing as a perfect essay. The prescribed format—introduction, thesis statement, body paragraphs, and conclusion—is just the skeleton of the essay. As the writer, it is your job to create the rest of the essay by applying your own knowledge, insights, and personality. An essay is a way to convey an idea or opinion to readers, and if you use the basic structure in conjunction with your intelligence and voice, then you will be on your way to a great final product!

ABOUT RENA PATEL

I am a day student at The Webb Schools in Claremont, California. I am interested in pursuing a career in writing and hope to become a successful author. I am also very interested in medicine and might like to become a psychiatrist. I have a passion for singing, cultivated by being in the choir and advanced choir in middle school. At Webb, I continued my love of singing by joining the chorus in my freshman year and then auditioning and being accepted into the school's Chamber Singers choir. In my sophomore year, I started the Indian Culture Club in order to give my campus and its students a taste of my heritage. That same year, I also started the Literary Club in hopes of reviving Webb's literary magazine and inspiring others to love literature as much as I do. I also play tennis and am a member of Webb's theater department as both an actress and a technician.

CHAPTER 15
Final Exams:
A Necessary (and Unfortunate)
Part of Life

by Yada Pruksachatkun
THINK Global School, Traveling International Boarding School—
Class of 2014
Hometown: Chiang Mai, Thailand

Ah yes, it's that time again. When waves of stress begin to suffocate you and your eyes dry up when thinking about the all-nighters and cups of coffee looming just beyond the horizon. Two words, three syllables. A concept that grows more palpable with each passing day. A phrase so feared by some that, with prayers merely bringing a false sense of security, only procrastination provides a source of escape.

Finals week.

As a student at the THINK Global School, a traveling boarding school, I have learned to deal with exams in a more productive manner. Here are the ways that I prepare, as well as some tips that will hopefully make *your* finals week a lot less stressful.

In the weeks leading up to any major examination, one might find up to ten pieces of paper taped around my room. For example, the first thing people would usually notice when walking into my room last spring term was a piece of posterboard taped above my desk, which read:

> *July 3: Math final, Spanish final*
>
> *July 4: History final*
>
> *July 5: Biology final*
>
> *July 6: English final*

Those dates stared down at me for the entire term, gradually imprinting themselves into my brain. By finals week, I was fully invested in those dates and ready to ace my exams.

Right beside it was another handwritten poster, this one for motivation. It read, "You know what you want, *carpe diem!*" And near these posters is my alarm, which goes off with an inspirational pop song every weekday at 6:30 a.m. It is with this alarm that I have learned one of the most important lessons when it comes to test prep—and studying in general: *Nothing is more important than sleep.* Less sleep equals more coffee, more coffee makes for tiredness later in the day, and tiredness turns into sloppy and rushed studying. There was a time when I never went to bed earlier than 2 a.m., but the quality of my schoolwork and studying suffered dramatically. Now, instead of cramming until the break of dawn before a test, I discipline myself to get to sleep earlier and to be well-rested for an exam.

One way I do this is by limiting my TV watching. During school terms, I deprive myself of television, for I have found TV to be addicting. Every time I've said, "I'm only going to watch one episode…" has ended up resulting in a midnight screening. The next day, I'm not only tired, but I'm more focused on last night's TV show than on my classes!

In addition to getting enough sleep, interacting with teachers can also help boost test grades. My computer has a schedule with the teachers' office hours perpetually up on my screen. Unfortunately, some of my teachers have office hours when I have classes, so when I can't see them in person, I just send them e-mails with all my questions. While it's the teacher's job to help students understand the subject matter, it's the student's responsibility to take the initiative when a concept or topic is confusing. Asking questions and gaining understanding is far better than holding back for fear of asking a seemingly stupid question.

When studying, you need to take your personality into account. Are you an introvert or an extrovert? I'm an introvert learner, and therefore, my study plan includes audio recordings of the material, a lot of homework music, and information visualization in solitude. For extroverts, study groups may be a way to interact with others and still get studying done. Groups are most effective when they review both the curriculum syllabus and former examinations. These are equally useful, as the former shows what students are expected to know and the latter gives actual questions and varying levels of difficulty. Group members can also help fill in the gaps in other members' knowledge. Tutoring one another in study groups is a good way for students to review what they know—or discover what they don't know.

Because learning is simply the act of making connections between preexisting materials, there can be many ways of learning the same thing. For instance, if you're an audio learner, make up a song about what you're learning. I once created a song about World War I's key dates, and that really helped me out at exam time. If you're a kinesthetic learner, try using hand movements to remember what you're saying. For example, I like to transcribe digital notes into handwriting, read the notes aloud, and then rewrite the notes again without looking at the digital version. Though time-consuming, the result is a comprehensive recollection of the dates, sequences, or mathematical equations on the test.

In addition, use technology to your benefit, not your detriment. Remember, you can be your own worst enemy. These days it's far too easy to succumb to the temptations of the Internet. That's why I use a few trusty applications and websites on my laptop to keep me focused. Some of my favorites are RescueTime, OmmWriter, and WhiteRoom; try using them to stay in the productive zone. RescueTime acts like Big Brother, tracking your web activities and reporting them to you in your e-mail every day. It's the equivalent of keeping a food diary, but it tracks digital (rather than food-based) distractions. OmmWriter is an audio-visual writing app that has different music and writing backgrounds to use. WhiteRoom is an app that shuts down all of your computer functions except for writing, so that's the last resort if you really cannot focus. If you like to study with music, you might find 8tracks useful. 8tracks is a Pandora-esque website with Internet playlists, and searching "finals + (your music genre preference)" will generate a hundred different results. If you have a smartphone or voice recorder, try recording yourself reciting your Spanish vocabulary or reviewing StudyBlue or Quizlet flashcards. If you have a Mac computer and an iPhone, Evernote is an amazing multi-device app that allows you to transfer entire documents from one device to another.

And last but not least, have some downtime! Two hours of hard studying and an hour of relaxing is better than 3 hours of distracted studying. For those times when I've studied so much my brain cannot process any more, a guitar, piano, or dancing shoes usually provide temporary relief. Even in the midst of finals week, make sure you always have an hour or two when you don't think about exams.

Instead of ending by saying that all the hard work will pay off in the end no matter what, I'm going to be honest: The effort doesn't always yield the results you want. All this preparation may work for some but not for others. You may feel like shredding your academic papers into tiny pieces after an unsuccessful finals week, but remember your reason for powering through high school, whatever it may be. Never lose this vision, but at the same time, realize that school is the ideal time and place for learning. And, if you've given all you have to studying and you're able to look through the syllabus before an exam and confidently say, "I've got it," then even if your grades may be lower than expected, you can be assured that you have succeeded. You've learned, and grades aside, that's all that really counts.

Yada's Rules for Acing Exams

Rule #1: Start reminding yourself of major tests weeks before the test days, especially if they are your finals.

Rule #2: Have a goal in mind. What is the payoff for all your hard work?

Rule #3: Don't be shy to ask your teachers questions.

Rule #4: Use the curriculum syllabus and former examinations as study guides.

Rule #5: Helping others study is a great way to help you review concepts.

Rule #6: Use technology to help you—don't let it hinder you.

Rule #7: Don't be a robot. Spend some time turning off your brain or doing something fun for a study break.

ABOUT YADA PRUKSACHATKUN

I am an award-winning creative writer and have travelled to over thirty-five countries in my young life. I attend the THINK Global School, the first traveling high school in the world. I enjoy aerial yoga, have started my own dance initiative to empower hospital children in Chiang Mai and abroad, and dabble in foreign languages. I chose to go to boarding school in order to really take my education—about which I am very passionate—to the next, more holistic level. At my school, I spread awareness for human rights as the co-founder of Wrists for Rights, participate in worldwide online think tanks with other high school students via the World Wide Think Tank, and help publish my school's e-magazine. I am also part of the music and photography clubs. If you want to read more from me, visit my blog: uforunspoken.com.

CHAPTER 16
Boarding School Athletics: Breaking a Sweat

by Amanda Reisman
Choate Rosemary Hall—Wallingford, Connecticut—Class of 2016
Hometown: Short Hills, New Jersey

Boarding school is a great place for students to discover their strengths and weaknesses and be challenged to reach their fullest potential. And that doesn't just apply to academics. Athletic activity is another tangible way to measure hard work and improvement, and it often plays a vital role in boarding school life.

When I first looked into boarding schools, I was awestruck. I had a hard time deciding which schools had the best balance of academics and athletics, an essential for any school I would consider. I ended up applying to four schools that, in my opinion, were strong both athletically and academically. Ice hockey is my main sport, so I needed to make sure that the school I would be going to had high-level hockey. During the application process, I met with the coaches of the ice hockey team at each school. After I was admitted, meeting the players and attending revisit days helped me narrow my choices down to one school. By the time I chose Choate, my research made me feel confident that I had found the right school for me.

At my school, every freshman is required to play three sports (one every term). Sports at boarding schools are different from what you may think. Dance, theater, and stagecraft are considered "non-sweat" sports. Throughout this chapter, I will be discussing and referring to traditional sports, which are also known as the "sweat" sports at my school. At most schools, there are different levels for each sport. Almost all sports offer varsity and junior varsity teams, and some even have a thirds team (one level below junior varsity). Most sports teams—all of the higher level teams—practice Monday, Tuesday, Thursday, and Friday after school for 1 to 2 hours. Each team has games on Wednesday and Saturday. At the end of each term, varsity teams (and some JV teams) can take part in the New England Championship Playoffs to determine the best in each sport out of all the competing prep schools in New England.

Tryouts start at the beginning of each term or sport season. Even if you made the team the year before, you still must try out. During tryouts, don't put too much pressure on yourself, but always try your very best. You don't have to stand out, but you should play to your potential. Coaches respect candidates who show 100 percent effort. Punctuality to tryouts is extremely important because the tryout is the first impression that you make on the coach. As the old saying goes, you never get a second chance to make a first impression! The very first day of ice hockey tryouts, I showed up in the locker room exactly on time, and my coach did not look pleased. Staring me down, she coldly remarked, "I can't stand it when people are late." I was scared to further disappoint my coach, so from that point on, I made it a priority to be present 15 minutes before every practice, game, and team event. You should learn from my mistake, and as far as athletics are concerned, always be early!

Every athlete knows that one of the most devastating moments in any athletic career is getting cut from a team. We all believe that we deserve a spot on the team, but only hard work, time, and effort can get us there. If you do get cut from a team, don't feel too disappointed—you will probably have another chance to make the team. Don't let being cut have a negative impact on your academics or your social life. And, of utmost importance, don't let this dampen your enthusiasm and commitment to that sport. Instead, let it be a wake-up call for you to try harder so that when tryouts come again next year, you will be even more eager (and prepared) to earn your place on the team. Display your determination to make the team through practice and effort.

Once on the team, every athlete must follow its rules and expectations. Whether you are a freshman or a senior, as a member of the team, you have a role that you must fill without hesitation. For me, joining a varsity team as a freshman was difficult but manageable. There were a lot of people to get to know, and there was a lot to learn. It wasn't always easy, but I did it … and so can you! Here are some tips to help you quickly feel like a part of the team.

Dress in your team's colors.

Another thing that your teammates and coaches take very seriously is dressing in your school's colors when you arrive for a game. More importantly, you shouldn't wear *any* garments of the opposing team's colors or your school rival's colors, or you will feel ashamed forever. When I was walking to the bus for my first away game, I realized everyone was glaring at me. I had made the mistake of wearing green—the school color of Choate's rival, Deerfield. I quickly learned to never do that again!

Don't complain ... Cheer!

Most freshmen at the varsity level receive little playing time. If you are one of those people, whatever you do, don't complain! Coaches notice this and obviously dislike it. Instead, show your enthusiasm and cheer for your team from the sidelines. If you do get playing time, try as hard as you can to do what you are asked to do and to play to your full potential. You don't want to let down your teammates and coaches. In addition, the seniors, captains, and coaches know what is best for the team. They are the most experienced and the wisest. They earned this superiority, so if they tell you to do something, then it's your duty to do it.

Be friendly!

When you first join the team, you may be a bit shy because you don't know anyone. It's crucial for you to try to make friends on your team. Understand that you might not be close with everyone on the team right away, but that's okay. Once you've made a few friends you'll soon feel like part of the team. One challenge that freshmen often encounter is learning everyone's name. At my first practice, people were quite offended when I called them by the wrong name. If you are unsure of someone's name, don't be afraid to ask!

Athletic teams have a hierarchy.

You must accept your role on the team, whether it's carrying the water bottles, sitting on the bench, or being a regular starter. Everyone has his or her own role, and if each person strives to succeed in their role then the team will succeed. Some team hierarchies are quite rigid. For example, the seniors get first pick of jersey numbers and lockers—followed by the juniors, then sophomores, and lastly, freshmen. First-year players typically do not get their first pick, but in coming years, their favorite numbers might be available. Despite this pecking order, it's important that you don't let the seniors take advantage of you. They shouldn't be able to push you around and command you to do everything. On the other hand, you may be responsible for remembering items to bring to games. Team managers sometimes handle this task, but some teams delegate these chores to the freshmen.

Sitting on the bench is something that all freshmen face at some point during the season or year. The older players are generally more experienced than most freshmen, so they get more playing time. If you (as a freshman) feel that you really deserve more playing time, you can politely discuss this with your coach—if you are on good terms with the coach, of course. Nobody expects the freshmen to carry the team. As long as you try your hardest, you will do fine. The older members of the team may be better than you, but the best players on the team are the ones who learn from the others and strive to reach their full potential. I look up to the captains on my team. I study why they are captains, and I try to mirror their play and attitude. I always ask myself, "How can I change my work ethic to become a better player, teammate, and leader?" Being a freshman on these teams has made me learn that you don't necessarily have to be a captain in order to be a leader and role model. The best players step up to the plate when needed, and they demonstrate hard work and perseverance all the time. Everyone should strive to be this kind of team member.

Develop meaningful relationships with your coaches.

Feeling comfortable with your coaches is very important. You need to be able to ask your coach personal questions. Coaches also dictate your playing time and can influence a college's decision to accept you or offer you a scholarship. They become your mentors and teachers of your sport. In addition, they know how to improve your skills and make you the best player, student, and person that you can be. For these reasons you should build a meaningful and personal relationship with your coaches.

Away games—there's a lot to remember!

When traveling to away games, be sure to bring the correct color uniform and make sure that you are punctual. In addition, it's always beneficial to bring homework on long bus trips, too, in order to stay on top of your schoolwork. You may want to bring headphones on the bus rides to away games to block out noise.

Academics before athletics.

Athletes at boarding schools have to give up some time in order to accommodate their sports. You'll also have to relinquish some social time on weekends to fit in homework, studying, and sports. Playing any varsity sport is very time consuming, so student-athletes at boarding schools must use their free time to do homework. On Sundays while at school, many committed athletes either train or play for their local club team. But make sure you do your schoolwork first!

Playing for a club team at boarding school may be difficult but not impossible if you're good at managing your time. I play for a club ice hockey team as well as my school team. I can't practice with my club team during the week because of school, but I can go to their games on Sundays. The biggest problem with this schedule was learning how to manage my time on the weekends in order to get my work done. While my friends were hanging out on Sunday nights, I was in the library studying. As an athlete, this is a choice that I have made.

Eat well!

In order to stay healthy, athletes must maintain a well-balanced diet. Even though the cookies and ice cream in the dining hall look amazing, you must train yourself to avoid them. Before you take a bite or lick, just think to yourself about all of the hard work that you have put into your sport and how indulging during the season could counteract your training.

Train, train, train!

Over the summer, get ahead on your athletics as well as your academics. Abide by the rigorous workout plan of a high-level high school athlete. Rise to the competition level and training level of your fellow teammates by training in the summer. In my freshman year at school, I distinctly remember being physically weaker than some of my older teammates. This summer, I've been going to the gym two or three times a week and have been on the ice two days a week. I've been training my mind, too—reading every day and doing SAT prep work two days a week. I know that this effort will help me become stronger, fitter, and more prepared for the next school year. If you haven't been training over the summer, then you're already behind and will need extra time to catch up to the others.

You should enjoy time with your teammates. Your sport will become your mental rest after a rigorous academic day. Don't worry about the little mistakes you make athletically. If you fall down, just get up and try again. If you miss the net, try again next time. If you don't make the team, try again next year. Just have fun with your sport. It's all worth it!

ABOUT AMANDA REISMAN

I've played ice hockey since I was 5 years old and decided to go to boarding school because the public high school in my town didn't offer this sport for girls. So I looked into, and eventually enrolled in, a boarding school that has both an excellent ice hockey program as well as rigorous academics. I played varsity field hockey, ice hockey, and lacrosse my freshman year. I am a member of the UNICEF Club and participate in the pop-skate program, a club designed to teach disabled children how to skate. In addition, I am a Gold Key tour guide for prospective students applying to Choate. I received the Edith Wallis award for the most contributions to athletics as a freshman, and I aspire to play ice hockey in college.

CHAPTER 17
Extracurricular Activities and Community Service: Outside Enrichment

by Coby Zur
The Lawrenceville School—Lawrence Township, NJ—Class of 2016
Hometown: Arrow Lakes, New Jersey

Entering boarding school in the fall of 2012 as a "II Former" (a ninth grader), I already had some expectations about how my high school career would unfold. From the research I had done, including school visits and conversations with faculty and students, I envisioned myself sitting with classmates around a Harkness table, dissecting and discussing the finer points of some book or historical event. I could almost hear the animated chants of "Go Big Red!" from the stands as my football teammates and I ran out onto the field to do battle on the gridiron. I pictured what it would be like to live in a house with my male peers, going through the daily routines of boarding school life. Yet, as I settled into my room at Thomas House ready to start preseason football practices in the week before classes began, I could not possibly have imagined that, just five months later, I would be debating foreign policy against two seniors from a rival school as well as playing a leading role in the Periwig Club (no, not an association of toupee enthusiasts, but rather a performing arts group). These and other extracurricular activities have come to define my Lawrenceville experience perhaps more indelibly than any achievements in the academic and athletic realms. And none of them may have become such important pillars of my high school experience had it not been for the opportunities presented at Lawrenceville's Club Night.

In mid-September, the entire Lawrenceville freshman class was required to attend Club Night in the Field House. I headed over as anything but a blank slate. I was completely certain about what I was—and was not—planning to do, and which clubs I would be joining. Or at least I thought I was certain about this.

I walked into the building, confident with my predetermined selections. My conviction weakened and my excitement grew as I inspected the various booths, featuring a dizzying array of options. Whenever I stumbled upon a club that piqued my interest, I decided to talk to its president and faculty advisor. Any reservations I may have had on my way to Club Night were swept away by impassioned descriptions of clubs and their mission statements. As a result, I left in a happy fog, a proud member of some fourteen clubs!

Returning to my freshman dormitory that night, several of my classmates asked me the familiar question: "What clubs did you join?" I answered with a straight face every time, rattling off the names of all fourteen clubs. Some of my housemates applauded my courage, others thought I was a complete "try-hard," and the smartest among them told me that I was flat-out insane. I laughed off all of their comments with a casual nonchalance. I mean, I could handle it; I could handle anything. And for the first few months, I actually did. Sure, I was being stretched a little thin and run a bit ragged, but I was powering through both my challenging course work and opposing offensive linemen. Even with these commitments, I was still able to attend every (yes, every!) club meeting, from the Japanese Language and Culture Club (armed with my ten-word Japanese vocabulary cultivated while reading James Clavell's *Shogun* and *Gai-Jin*), to the Philosophy Club (did it even matter if I showed up?), to both the Arabic Culture Society and Jewish Students Organization (since I thought I could solve the Arab-Israeli conflict in my spare time).

I made it through the first term with my sanity intact, barely. When I hopped back into the ring for winter term, I was coming back to a new world. Football had given way to wrestling, a sport with which I had no prior experience. Whereas before I had a free period, in this term my classmates and I now had an additional course added to our schedules, and in all of my classes the workload and difficulty levels increased. On top of all of that, I had auditioned for and landed the lead role of Brutus in the II Form production of *Julius Caesar.* Just one week with my crazy schedule proved to be considerably more than I could handle. I was forced to sit down that weekend and cross one club after another off my list. Honing in on the clubs and involvements that excited me most was an important exercise, as it enabled me to have a fulfilling and productive year, and it set the tone for the years to come.

Looking back on it now, I can see that I had fallen prey to a common pitfall that can prevent a student from maximizing his or her boarding school experience. My term for what I experienced is "Kid in a Candy Store Syndrome." As you look ahead to your own boarding school experience, you may relate to my story, or you may find yourself in another scenario that could trip you up.

MISCONCEPTIONS ABOUT EXTRACURRICULAR INVOLVEMENT

Here is my short list of these misconceptions, starting with my own predicament:

Kid in a Candy Store Syndrome: *"All these clubs look great, so I'll just join them all. I'm sure I can handle it."* Some of you may be coming from middle schools that have limited extracurricular programs, as was the case for me. Even though the wide array of activities may be a breath of fresh air, I urge you not to bite off more than you can chew. You'll find that dedicating yourself to a handful of clubs that you really enjoy is more valuable and rewarding than trying to take on too many.

Means to an End Malaise: *"These clubs would look great on my college résumé, so I guess I should join them."* While you may be very focused on your future, you won't benefit as much as you hope from such an approach. First of all, if you don't really like the clubs in which you are a member, you are less likely to be fully involved in the club's activities and leadership possibilities. It actually looks more impressive (and is a lot more fun) to devote three or four years to a club that truly interests you and then become a leader in that club, rather than attaching your name to many prestigious clubs that don't really resonate with you.

Mission Impossible Disorder: *"Boarding school is going to be tough enough as is; I definitely won't be able to handle any extracurriculars."* One of the amazing advantages of boarding school is that with so many clubs and programs available at every turn, students are presented with the chance to explore who they are, figure out who they want to be, and express themselves. These opportunities are wasted, however, if you don't capitalize on them. Take a leap, try something that looks interesting. If you manage your time well, you'll find that you're able to squeeze in a meeting or two and will be the better for it.

Equally important as special-interest clubs, community service provides an outlet to help those in need both locally and globally. Some schools have a community service requirement (my school mandates 40 hours in the sophomore and junior years). If your school does not have such a requirement, I still highly recommend that you participate in a program that allows you to give back to the community. There may be some clubs on campus already focused on nonprofit work, and you can always ask the community service director at your school for ways to involve yourself in volunteer efforts.

I spent the first term of my boarding school career so caught up in my own activities that I neglected to think of others beyond the Lawrenceville campus. Two weeks before Christmas, our community service representative stood up asking for volunteers to chaperone local underprivileged children at a holiday party we were hosting on campus. I decided to sign up, but without much enthusiasm. When he came to me a couple of days later asking me to elevate my role from chaperone to Santa Claus, I hesitated. But after being informed that I was the only volunteer tall enough to fit into the adult costume, I stepped up to the challenge of being the first and hopefully best Jewish Santa Claus ever to don the white beard! Seeing the looks on the little kids' faces as I entered the room with the iconic red bag slung over my shoulder showed me how much a small act of kindness could impact others' lives. Since then, I have jumped at other chances to volunteer in community service efforts, from renovating a local public school for Jersey Cares to planting a garden in an at-risk neighborhood in Trenton.

The college counselors at Lawrenceville do not speak to Underformers (ninth and tenth graders) about what students can do specifically to prepare for college. Instead they advise students to "do Lawrenceville well." This means not trying to boost your credentials for the admissions process, but rather making the most out of your high school career by immersing yourself in every facet of boarding school life. You only have one chance to do boarding school well, so jump in with both feet. If there's a club that looks cool, join it. If there's an activity that intrigues you, sign up for it. If you think there's something you would like to do that isn't offered, start your own club—all it may take is one or two other students who share your interest and a teacher willing to serve as an advisor. If well-balanced, your extracurricular experience may prove to be the most valuable and formative component of your time on campus.

Boarding School Quiz

For those of you already attending boarding school, here's a little quiz to see how you are faring in the effort to balance your extracurricular involvement*:

1. Sleep is:

   a. Inconvenient

   b. Sweet, sweet nectar

   c. Sleep? What's that?

2. I am a member of _____ clubs:

   a. 6 to 10

   b. 1 to 5

   c. Umm, carry the two…let me count again

3. Community service is:

   a. Commendable

   b. A valuable and fulfilling endeavor

   c. A frivolous waste of time

4. When I think about my upcoming club meetings, I feel:

   a. Stressed but under control

   b. Happy and excited

   c. Dread and bile rising in my throat

Disclaimer: This is by no means an accurate assessment of your extracurricular success. Consult an expert (like your parents) if you are seeking an actual advisory opinion.

Scoring:

Each "**a.**" response is worth 1 point, "**b.**" responses are worth 2 points, and "**c.**" responses are worth 0.

If you scored 6 to 8 points, you seem to have struck a good balance, keep it up!

If you scored 3 to 5 points, you are hanging in there, but try to find the joy in your various activities. If something is causing you stress, you may need to consider whether it is in your best interest to keep so many commitments.

If you scored 0 to 2…I pray for you.

ABOUT COBY ZUR

I have always been independent by nature. I like doing things for myself and saw boarding school as a perfect environment where this personality trait could be nurtured. I felt that boarding school offered a warm and supportive administrative system with the right balance between freedom and guidance when needed. The close-knit social structure, encompassing both students and faculty, also appealed to me, and the unique combination of innovative academics and competitive sports programs further convinced me that I belonged at boarding school. At Lawrenceville, I am on the football and wrestling teams, participate in theater, and am a member of many clubs: Periwig Club, Calliopean Society (political discussion and analysis group), Speech and Debate, Jewish Students Organization, IMPULSE (improv troupe), Adrenaline Club, and the Philosophy Club.

CHAPTER 18
Money Management:
Handling Your Finances

by Andrew Granato
Middlesex School—Concord, Massachusetts—Class of 2013
Hometown: Bexley, Ohio

While there can be a lot of challenging experiences related to boarding school, handling money doesn't have to be one of them. Most issues with regard to spending money on (and off) campus are logistical issues and aren't really too much trouble. As a student who receives financial aid at my boarding school, I've become adept at managing my finances while still juggling the other, more interesting aspects of boarding school life. Here are some of the common fiscal issues you may encounter when living away from home.

SECURITY

Pretty much everyone at my boarding school has some cash on hand, either in their wallets or in their rooms. Middlesex provides a safe in every room for a student's money, passport, and other items, and I know of some other boarding schools that do the same. If your school doesn't, you should find a secure hiding place (such as tucked away in a dresser drawer or hidden in an old coat pocket in the back of your closet) for your valuables. Your hiding spot should do a good job of keeping your items secure.

Usually when there's theft at a boarding school, it involves food left in the communal fridge—especially in boys' dorms, it's generally open season on anything left in there. However, I can remember one time where there was a more serious issue with a thief in my dorm. Someone was taking money and other valuables that had been left out on students' desks. Issues like this should be handled by reporting all thefts to your dorm faculty, who have no doubt dealt with such issues in the past and will probably call a dorm meeting on the subject. They'll also keep an eye out for anything suspicious and alert others to what happened. The robber in my dorm was eventually caught and the money returned because one of the victims went to his house counselor, who threatened to invoke serious punishment unless the thief turned himself in. That said, the easiest and best preventative measure is to remember to lock your door. I always kept my door locked whenever I left my room, and nothing ever happened to me. Moreover, if you're planning to bring a significant amount of money to campus (more on that later), keep the bulk of it in your safe or hiding place and carry only a few dollars with you, just to be safe. I know this isn't fun to talk about, but take these few commonsense security measures and you should be fine. Again, except for the fridge stuff, theft is very rare at Middlesex, and I've never heard of any boarding school that has a reputation for being unsafe.

CASH, CARDS, STUDENT ACCOUNTS, AND QUARTERS

Most people at Middlesex have access to a couple of sources of money. Some parents give their child some sort of cash allowance, others have a tacit agreement that the student can access the family credit card as long as he or she doesn't spend too much, and many utilize both methods. Cash is useful if there's some sort of school fundraiser, which happens at Middlesex about once a month. Credit and debit cards are primarily used to order food online or go into town. Most boarding schools also employ some sort of school account into which your parents deposit money that you can use for textbooks or at the school store. Middlesex's school store has all of the standard things found at any on-campus school store: toiletries (toothpaste, deodorant, etc.), school supplies (pencils, notebooks, etc.), and school spirit wear (sweatshirts, sweatpants, scarves, leggings, and other assorted clothing items). Finally, make sure to bring plenty of quarters for the laundry machines. Change is sometimes hard to come by, and you don't want to be stuck without a way to clean your clothes!

"NEITHER A BORROWER NOR A LENDER BE"

I recommend that you try to avoid borrowing or lending money as much as possible. It's practically a running joke in a high school dorm that irresponsible guys (and girls, too!) will forget that they don't have money on them when they order food, so they need to run around the dorm, begging someone else for money and promising to pay them back. Occasionally, this develops into drama—someone claims that he or she paid the other person back, but the other person disagrees, and it quickly escalates into a mess. There's no faster way to build tension between two people than to involve misplaced money, and it's easier (and a relief to everyone) if people just pay for their own stuff. Yeah, maybe at some point you'll need to borrow a few bucks, but don't make a habit of it. I once had an agreement with a friend that, whenever we ordered food, we would alternate paying for it to make the payment process more simple, and that worked pretty well. If you're going to be spending money on a semi-regular basis, you might want to try that sort of arrangement.

HOW BOARDING STUDENTS TYPICALLY SPEND MONEY

As I mentioned before, the school store has all of the basics for survival, and you won't really need to go off campus for much. For me and most of the people I know, off-campus food is the biggest drain on our finances. Middlesex is a great school in many ways, but its food is not a strong point. This is a common complaint among boarding students everywhere, not just those at Middlesex. A school's food is typically edible and decently diverse, but sometimes you just have to have something more. At Middlesex, there are a couple of options for buying food that isn't on the meal plan. You can go to The Grill, an on-campus eatery open during certain afternoon and evening hours and run by the same company that provides the normal dining service. The food at The Grill is generally better than at the dining hall and more like the food that you'd find at a sports concession stand (hamburgers, soda, calzones, and so on). You can also order food from a few local restaurants. Judging by the money Middlesex students funnel into them, these establishments must love us! You can also go into town. Middlesex is located in Concord, Massachusetts, a quintessential small New England town. It has all the usual places: coffee shops, restaurants, a CVS pharmacy, a grocery store, and a library. Obviously, depending on the school you attend, this will be different, but most boarding schools have access to some off-campus shopping options.

On weekends, students can also go into Boston, which is a little over a half hour away. Obviously, Boston has everything, and though I almost never went there as a student, I know of a couple of kids who liked to go once or twice a month. Also, with Amazon, an entire world of nonperishable goods is as close as your laptop or smartphone and can be delivered to your dorm in just a few days. That said, you honestly can go an entire year at boarding school spending barely anything at all, and it's not a big deal. All I ever bought was food.

SOCIOECONOMICS OF MONEY

Finally, the subject of money can get awkward due to socioeconomic disparities at boarding school. The vast majority of boarding schools are located in or near extremely wealthy communities. I was on full financial aid at a school where roughly 30 percent of the student body receives some form of aid, and statistically, I'm a middle-class American. When a high school's tuition is roughly $50,000 a year, if you don't receive need-based financial aid, your family's income is probably in the top 5–10 percent in the United States. In everyday boarding school life, these disparities show up most often in the clothes people wear and how people talk about their families, homes, and vacations. For many low- and middle-income students, this can be a source of tension. So for all those at boarding school, I ask that students who come from wealthy families be sensitive to those concerns and try not to flaunt their resources (e.g., don't brag about expensive purchases). If finances are tight for you, don't be too hard on yourself or envious of others. Though it might not seem like it at first glance, there are many students on your campus whose situation is similar to yours. Most students on both ends of the financial spectrum deal with this disparity well, and because there isn't all that much to buy on a boarding school campus anyway, this isn't often an issue. Just have common sense about it and be aware of how you present yourself, and there shouldn't be too much awkwardness.

Those are some of the basic guidelines for dealing with personal finance at boarding school. If you have more specific questions, ask older students (preferably with a similar financial status as yours) or dorm faculty members about how money is normally handled at your school. They're there to help and are experienced in this aspect of boarding school life. Have fun at boarding school!

ABOUT ANDREW GRANATO

I was born in Iowa City, Iowa, and moved to Bexley, Ohio, when I was seven. I attended public schools until ninth grade, when I became so frustrated with my school system's bureaucracy and attitude towards grade acceleration that I applied to several boarding schools on the East Coast. I chose Middlesex because it gave me the most financial aid. Not really knowing much about Middlesex at all (beyond that I wanted to leave my hometown), I was fortunate to end up at a school that offered pretty much everything I wanted out of my high school education. I'll always be grateful to Middlesex for the opportunities it provided me, and I'm glad to be a representative for the school. At Middlesex, I served as a community service officer, women's lacrosse manager, assistant in the athletic office, dorm proctor, peer tutor, co-head of Model Congress, vice president of JSA (Junior Statesmen of America), and a minor head of the Finance Club. I was also a member of GSA (Gay Straight Alliance), Short Story Society, the boys' junior varsity cross-country team, and Chamber Ensemble, where I played violin and viola. I now attend college at Stanford University.

CHAPTER 19
Nutrition: Healthy Meals, Dining Hall Choices, and Snacks

by Zoha Qamar
Phillips Exeter Academy—Exeter, New Hampshire—Class of 2015
Hometown: Rancho Cucamonga, California

A s the saying goes, some eat to live, while others live to eat. Regardless of where you fall on this spectrum, eating is an integral part of life. At boarding school, food serves as a means of socializing with others, comforting yourself during stressful times, and properly fueling your body to optimize your overall experience. Though each school provides different options in dining halls, town eateries, and grocery stores, food is an important aspect of any boarding school. After all, boarding school is populated by several hundred hungry teenagers!

MAKING SMART CHOICES

It feels as though food influences almost everything at Exeter. It establishes motivation, comfort, power, a currency, and even memories. Clubs and forums, for example, almost always conclude announcements and e-mails with "There will be food." And I've found that food permeates my life even more directly. One of my favorite nights of this past school year was Super Bowl night in my dorm, Langdell Hall. The dorm faculty set up a spread of chips, cheese, and every topping imaginable for a microwaveable nacho night in our common room. Thank you, Langdell Hall, because that seriously rocked.

Regrettably, not every night is nacho night; despite this, food is always easily accessible. Dining halls are generally open from the early morning to about dorm check-in time. After a few weeks at school, you'll get a feel for the dining hall's menu rotations and get to know which food items you like and dislike. If you tend to be picky, eat well during the meals you enjoy. This also helps curb the temptation of late-night snacking. As soothing as midnight ramen can be, it's really not a positive habit. If you do like the occasional midnight snack, you can take a couple pieces of fruit from the dining hall back to your room that evening. When used for a study snack, bananas taste a lot better than you think.

Even if a school's dining quality is top-notch, it's unlikely that you'll love all the meals offered. Use a little creativity and experiment at mealtimes to create something you like. I haven't perfected the recipe, but some students have discovered ways to make their own pizzas with pita, marinara sauce, and cheese. On the other hand, I swear by making my own egg salad with the salad bar's hard-boiled eggs and add-ins from the sandwich bar. While not every meal is a hit, there is always enough food at dining halls to ensure that students don't go hungry. A boarder's main reason to dislike dining hall food is that it doesn't always measure up to our memories of home-cooked food. Still, this builds a little character and is part of the boarding experience.

Even if you really like your dining hall, it's always nice to order in or eat out occasionally. Exeter, New Hampshire, is a small town compared to my hometown in Southern California, but it still offers the luxury of restaurant access. On the days that the dining hall's selection doesn't suit my liking, I'll sometimes head to town for avocado rolls, calzones, or steak burritos (my personal local favorites). As I've come to realize, outside food is a genuine source of excitement. Take a look at the restaurants in your town and begin noting your favorites.

If there are any grocery stores, convenience stores, or pharmacy stores in your vicinity, definitely make use of them. They are ideal for stocking up on food for late-night snacks or to find comforts from home—in the form of processed and nonperishable goods—that aren't available in your dining hall.

AVOIDING THOSE EXTRA POUNDS

Gaining weight is a concern for many students, especially for freshmen and other first years. If you're worried about your weight, being conscious is the first step in avoiding putting on extra pounds. For most students, this is their first time away from home, where their diets were at least somewhat controlled. They need to develop an awareness of their own eating habits. Athletic requirements help keep students active, and most schools also have some sort of health classes. Still, tri-varsity athletes and those who simply meet the minimum athletic requirements typically have distinctly different food needs and levels of diet awareness. Even individuals within each group have varying levels of food intake and concern about gaining weight. Other factors, like personal habits and metabolism, can also impact weight. But being healthy is about being smart, so maintain that mindset and consider replacing the late-night snack binge with a trip to the gym instead. But as long as you're not gorging on fast food and candy bars every day of the week, you should be fine.

EXPERIMENTING AND DIVERSIFYING

Boarding school is a place where you can delve into unfamiliar and engaging academic, athletic, and social settings. And it's also a great opportunity to immerse yourself in your friends' diverse dietary norms and experiment with new food choices as well. My vegetarian friend Liddy, who is very pro–fruits and veggies, once convinced me to walk a mile and a half to the Stop & Shop supermarket to buy chocolate chips, strawberries, and a coconut. It was easy to microwave the chocolate and dip the strawberries, but neither of us had ever attempted to open a coconut at school. We tried a knife, but to no avail, so we ultimately walked out onto the quad and cracked it open. Then, to our delight, we learned that chocolate coconut was quite a treat. That next weekend, we walked back to the Stop & Shop, just for the coconut and chocolate, and we shattered it open on the quad once again, very pleased with our new culinary discovery.

Although I am not Jewish, I observed Passover this year with Cornelia, one of my best friends. Boarding school provides an opportunity to embrace other traditions and dive into new experiences, so I figured that if I've celebrated Ramadan my whole life, I could try another form of fasting. It's safe to say that eliminating leavened goods from my diet and keeping kosher for a whole week proved to be more challenging than I had imagined. After we skipped baked desserts in the dining hall for a few days, Cornelia found an online recipe for Passover-friendly chocolate chip cookies and immediately convinced me to make the treats that weekend. After trips to both Walgreens and the Stop & Shop, we found ourselves in the Student Center's kitchen that Sunday afternoon.

Since we had passed up cakes, pies, and cookies that whole week, the thought of chocolate chip cookies had us enthralled. While beginning to mix the batter, we quickly ignored the thin-with-lumps consistency, surmising that it was probably the matzo meal. As we dolloped dough onto cookie sheets, the pallid dough sections began running into each other, but we nevertheless happily slid the first pan into the oven. With the temperature at 350° and the timer set for 14 minutes, Cornelia and I eagerly hovered nearby. Our impatience quickly won out, so we tugged lightly at the door handle to sneak a peek. Black crust, liquid center. Dry ashes framed the edges of the pan, watery dough soaked the remaining area, and chocolate chunks were scattered across the pan. I snatched an oven mitt and slammed the pan onto the stove to cool. After giving the remaining "dough" a second stir, we finally acknowledged something had seriously gone wrong.

Recognizing that our batter was much too thin, Cornelia added some more matzo meal and attempted to bake it again. Meanwhile, I oiled a pan and began frying that thin, remaining center from our first attempt into a few pancakes. We did our best to salvage our effort, but not everyone back in the dorm was a fan of our final creation. While I actually liked the matzo-chocolate-chip-pancakes, the experience of attempting to make them was much better than any cookie we could have baked. And, thus, Passover prompted me to further my religious knowledge, test my self-restraint, and refine my appreciation for real, soft, leavened bread.

KEEPING FOOD AND SNACKS IN YOUR ROOM

Though our matzo cookies did not end up perfectly, there is one thing at Exeter that always seems to have a perfect outcome: receiving an e-mail notifying you of a special surprise waiting in the mailroom. The ultimate jackpot at boarding school is receiving a package, especially a care package with food. Varying widely in size and containing anything (or any food) from anyone, these boxes can brighten your day, week, and potentially life. Family and friends from home often want to support and keep in touch with you while you are away, and there is no better way than care packages! Food, blankets, food, books, food—we love it all. Once you get all this food, though, you need to store it. To keep everything fresh, Ziploc® bags never fail. Use them to prevent your Goldfish® crackers from going stale, or throw your extra cup of dry Raisin Bran® in a bag for later.

When you keep food in your room, just-add-water items are convenient, cheap, and tasty. Granted, they're not the healthiest options, but it's almost impossible to go through your boarding school career without eating a convenient Cup O'Noodles® or two. Some choose microwaveable mac and cheese, others are ramen purists, and a few people even keep microwaveable Indian food, so it depends on what you want and what you can store. Dorms may also have what Exonians refer to as "dorm grill," a program run by students or faculty that allows you to purchase food in your dorm during specified hours on certain days.

Although you should primarily stock up on food that you like for your room, know that cereal and other breakfast items are always helpful to have. Late nights are inevitable at boarding school, and squeezing in a few extra minutes of sleep by skipping breakfast is often appealing. Ideally, waking up in time to have your morning meal in the dining hall every day is healthy and helps maintain a steady schedule, but realistically, there will be days where sleep trumps any thoughts of eggs or yogurt. On these days, a handful of Life® or Frosted Flakes® cereal on your way to class makes a world of difference.

When it comes to storing perishable food, like the leftovers from last weekend, you should probably use your dorm's common fridge. Unfortunately, food theft sometimes happens. Dorms address these issues when they occur, but preventing them in the first place is best. Try avoiding this heart-breaking fate by storing your fridge goods in paper bags or lunchboxes; it may not be 100 percent foolproof, but it wards off a fair number of scavengers. Some schools allow personal mini-fridges in student rooms, although this is usually only allowed for medical reasons. If you're interested in fridges, hotpots, or other such equipment for your room, check your school's policy before making a purchase.

EXPERIENCE THE LOCAL CUISINE

Day students can also heavily influence your culinary experience at boarding school. Beyond being classmates, teammates, and friends, they are a great resource for recommending restaurants in the area, or better yet, offering an invitation to their homes for a long-awaited, home-cooked meal. Similarly, when your parents visit, make sure to eat at your favorite restaurants and consider bringing some friends along. Inviting friends makes for good dinner conversation and is a nice thing to do. Who knows, when their parents are in town, they might return the favor!

A FINAL THOUGHT

Food at Exeter has both nurtured me physically and taught me to be resourceful, creative, and adventurous. And with every break, I appreciate my mom's food more and more.

ABOUT ZOHA QAMAR

I began ninth grade at Phillips Exeter Academy in the fall of 2011. I love to try new foods, new sports, and new books. Fluent in three languages and conversational in two, I am always looking for the next international travel opportunity. I enjoy writing opinion pieces for PEA's newspaper *The Exonian,* programming my latest idea, and spending time in Langdell Hall, my dorm. Having loved my experience at Exeter thus far, I strongly believe that success at boarding school relies on your capability to balance poise and fearfulness, to open your eyes and mind along with your arms, and to embrace the emotions and unknowns you'll inevitably encounter.

CHAPTER 20
Social Life: Friends, Dating, and Having Fun

by Sarah Rudkin
Fay School— South Borough, Massachusetts
The Taft School—Watertown, Connecticut—Class of 2010
Tilton School (Postgraduate)—Tilton, New Hampshire
Hometown: Camarillo, California and Jimbaran, Bali

Being away from the comforts of home is always tough, and factoring in the awkwardness that comes with adolescence further complicates things. When preparing to go to boarding school, you'll invariably have a number of social worries: Will I make new friends? Will I even fit in? Will I be the only person in my grade without a boyfriend or girlfriend? Will I embarrass myself in front of the whole school? The list is endless. Your parents have probably told you to just be yourself and you will find your place in life, but you've likely shrugged it off multiple times as a typical parental platitude and don't want to heed the advice. But no matter how much you may not like to admit it, I'm here to tell you that your parents are right. Being yourself means you'll find the people who share similar interests, opinions, and goals, so you won't have that awkward, forced feeling when trying to get to know them. Things will just flow naturally with these people, and you will find yourself feeling comfortable with them.

I spent most of my boarding school years at The Taft School in Connecticut. I entered as a sophomore, so it was a bit tougher because returning students already had their groups of friends, none of which I instantly clicked with. My wardrobe didn't consist of the clothes that most prep-school students wear (Lilly Pulitzer, J. Crew, Ralph Lauren, Vineyard Vines, Sperrys, and so on), and my skinny jeans, rock band t-shirts, Converse shoes, and dark-colored clothing didn't make the best first impression. My peers were hesitant to connect with me, especially since I had also just dyed my hair pink. I spent the first few days at Taft feeling utterly lost, homesick, and—above all else—lonely. On my third night there, my dormitory's fire alarm went off, and we all had to stand outside to wait for the fire department to come and turn it off. A few feet away from me was the red-headed girl who lived next to me but to whom I had only said "hi" once. She honestly scared me; she seemed to hate me instantly when I had walked into her room and introduced myself on move-in day. Now, outside in the cold, while all the other girls were wearing their pajamas, she was just in her towel, with shampoo still in her hair. She caught me looking at her, and I simply started laughing. The whole situation looked like something that should be in a comedy movie, not in real life at boarding school. She stared at me for a second and then started laughing with me, realizing how funny it was, too. That's how my friendship with her began. We became such good friends that, eventually, people would be confused or concerned if they saw one of us without the other.

I may not have been the person with the most friends at Taft, but I never tried to be someone I was not. Because of this, I made close friends, ones whom I still keep in touch with and visit. Most importantly, I became happy there. By being myself, not judging other students, getting involved in student life as a dormitory monitor in my junior year, joining the tennis team, and participating in clubs that I was passionate about, I was able to talk to and befriend people I wouldn't have otherwise. Unless you are that person who showers only once a week and can be smelled from ten feet away, I promise that out of all the students who attend your school, you will find at least one friend. Be brave and spontaneous. Boarding school is all about finding your strengths and weaknesses, overcoming your fears, and growing into the person you are meant to be. Every day will challenge you in different ways, but it all starts with the first step of reaching out and getting to know people. Go on, take this step, and you will soon find yourself having a great time at your school.

TIPS ON BOARDING SCHOOL SOCIAL LIFE

If you want to date someone seriously, go for it! If you want to stay single, go for it! Even if it seems like everyone else in your group of friends or grade is dating, don't feel pressured to do the same. A year or two down the road, it won't matter if some people thought you were "weird" for not doing what they were at a particular point in time. Do whatever feels comfortable for you.

When you're dating someone, don't be with them every waking moment of the day. When you live on the same campus as the person you are dating, you'll see them a lot without even trying. Don't suffocate yourselves with each other or the relationship can become strained very quickly. Learn how to balance personal time, time with your friends, and time with the person you are seeing.

Sure, you have feelings for this person. Sure, they have feelings for you. You have fun together, you laugh when you are with them, and you feel like the king or queen of the world when you're with them. But if your grades slip too far, you won't be able to continue going to the same school as that person. Boarding school is about becoming well-rounded. Don't let yourself fall into an extreme lifestyle of working exclusively on your social life or your study skills. Balance is key.

If your boarding school sweetheart finds someone else, don't go crazy. You'll be spending the next few years in proximity to him or her, so ending things badly will only cause you future distress and awkwardness. Save yourself the many months (and potentially years) of headaches trying to make sure your schedule doesn't coincide with his or hers. Simply end things in a respectful, mature way. Besides, you're at boarding school to learn how to grow, so apply it to all aspects of your life.

When at a school dance, you have the opportunity to let loose and have some fun. Go wild with your dance moves! Don't hold back—those school dances are few and far between. If you're the type of person who enjoys dancing with someone you like, by all means, do it. However, try to avoid mimicking the people in those twerking videos, even if others are doing it. It's awkward for everyone who has to look at the person who is making the situation a little too R-rated.

We all know that rumors can spread quickly, but at boarding school, they spread like wildfire. It may be tempting to partake in gossip sessions with friends (guys, don't even try saying you don't gossip—it isn't just girls who do it), but try to avoid it. Hurtful words, personal things that should have stayed personal, and blatant lies can spread. This makes for a divided and accusatory environment of "she said/he said," and you can lose some great friends or make someone feel betrayed as a result. That said, we all make mistakes sometimes. If you realize that you've hurt someone's feelings with something you said, you need to apologize and take responsibility for your actions.

Even though the boarding school you attend (or hope to attend) is probably known for its academic rigor, you should always find some time to get out of your room or the library. Especially on weekends, there should be plenty of social activities for you to enjoy. If you're bored on a Saturday night, attend a dance, movie night, game night, or another school-sponsored entertainment event. Sometimes boarding schools host some pretty famous public figures and interesting lecturers who are definitely worth seeing.

If you don't play on a sports team of your own, consider supporting your friends in their athletic endeavors when they're playing at home. If you're more of a theater person, attend your friends' plays, concerts, and other productions. By definition, parents are around much less frequently at boarding school than they would be at a day school. So it's important to cheer on your friends because, chances are, their parents and siblings aren't able to do so in person.

ABOUT SARAH RUDKIN

I was born in Jackson Hole, Wyoming, but I moved to Andorra when I was two. I then moved to Switzerland when I was four and lived there for fourteen years; this is where I consider home to truly be. After Switzerland, I moved to Bali, Indonesia, and I've been living here for the past four years. I went to boarding school because my father and his brothers went (St. George's and Phillips Andover), and I wanted to experience what my father talked about so fondly. I started at the age of eleven at Rumsey Hall for seventh grade, Fay School for eighth and ninth, The Taft School for tenth through twelfth, and Tilton School for a postgrad year. I was always involved in community service, the tennis and volleyball teams, horseback riding and competing in events off campus, the school newspaper, becoming a school monitor/proctor at Fay and Taft, and later the Lesbian, Gay, Bisexual, Transgender (LGBT) Club at Taft.

CHAPTER 21
Drugs, Alcohol, Hazing, Cheating, and Safety: The Heavy Stuff

by "Jane Doe"
Boarding School—U.S.A.—Class of 2015

A Note from Justin: The name of this chapter's author, the school she attends and its disciplinary committee and "turning-in" program, and other names used in this chapter have been changed to preserve anonymity and to allow the author to speak freely about this sensitive topic that is prevalent at all high schools—boarding or otherwise—across the United States. I am grateful for her honesty in addressing this universal topic of concern for students and their parents.

The summer before high school, I promised my mother I wouldn't drink. It started like this:

"So, Jane," my mom said, leaning against our kitchen counter. "School starts next week. Are you getting excited?"

I shrugged. I suppose I was a little excited, but I was also scared. Ultimately, though, I was trying very hard not to think about any of it.

"Oh, don't be too worried about it," she said. "You're going to have so much fun. I just need to make sure you're going to make good decisions. At boarding school, you'll have a lot more freedom. I'm not always going to be there. So, no alcohol, or anything, okay? You know that, right?"

I rolled my eyes. "Yes, Mom, I know."

"Promise me, okay?"

"I promise," I mumbled, not exactly sure what I was agreeing to. At that point, the boarding school I'd be living at in a few months was just a far-off collection of brick-and-ivy buildings, populated only with white-haired professors and deans. In my kitchen on a warm summer night, I couldn't imagine that going to this seemingly stiff and formal school would include alcohol and partying.

I even forgot about the promise, until one afternoon in early September.

"Hey, Jane. Mom talked to you about drinking and stuff, right?" said Abbey, my older sister who also attended the boarding school.

I nodded.

"Thought so. What did she say?"

"That I shouldn't," I replied. "And that I need to make good decisions."

Abbey turned her gaze to me.

"She's right, you know," she said, watching my face carefully.

I contemplated this. Just last weekend, some friends from middle school had gotten drunk at a high school party. I thought it really couldn't be that bad if some of my best friends were doing it.

Abbey must have seen the indecision flicker across my face, because she continued.

"Look, Jane. It's really just not worth it. It's bad for you, and if you got caught, you'd be throwing away such a good education. Plus, you don't need booze to have fun. Let's make a deal. We both won't drink or anything while we're at school. Okay?"

I paused. I'd been lectured about the dangers of teen drinking by parents and D.A.R.E. seminar leaders for years. But hearing it from my older sister, a peer who was going through everything I was, made not drinking seem a lot more realistic.

I nodded vigorously. "All right, deal," I said. Abbey grinned.

IT'S OKAY TO SAY "NO"

Fast forward a few months, and it's a Saturday night in the beginning of spring term. The weather was warm, and the morale on campus was high. Everyone had finally crawled out of their dorms and was outside, night bridge-jumping, playing hide-and-seek, licking ice-cream cones from the dining hall, and, above all, socializing. My friends and I were playing Ultimate Frisbee in a park on the outskirts of campus. When there was a lull in the game, Amanda slid a plastic bottle out of her backpack and began to pass it around.

"One of the day students gave it to me. I think she had to get rid of it or something. Oh, and I mixed it with orange juice, so it doesn't taste so bad anymore," she said, taking a quick sip.

"Jane, do you want some?"

I paused, a little curious about how the alcohol would burn my throat and blur my thoughts, and a little worried about what she would think of me if I said no.

But then I remembered Abbey's words and swallowed my hesitations.

"No thanks, Amanda. I don't really drink," I said, shifting my gaze from the ground to the trees to the sky and picking at a blade of grass.

"Oh yeah, no worries. I have some soda in my bag too," she said, drying a Coke on her shirt and tossing to me. I caught it and smiled, relaxing back into the grass.

It was weird, I thought. *Saying no had been easy.*

I hesitated to say no for the same reasons thousands of other high-schoolers hesitate: I was afraid. I was afraid of being labeled a killjoy, afraid of being teased, and afraid of being left out. But in reality, they respected my answer. In fact, based on my experiences, almost everyone respects the answer no. And if for some reason they don't, then they probably aren't the type of people you want as friends. It sounds really basic, but anywhere in life, and especially at boarding school, where the majority of your time is spent with peers, it's important to surround yourself with people who make you comfortable.

Sometimes, though, because of bad luck or poor timing, I've been in situations where simply saying "I don't drink" wasn't enough. It could be in a dorm setting, with upperclassmen offering a quick drink or smoke, or maybe after practice with a sports team. In high-pressure situations like this, it's important to have a few go-to responses. Blame it on parents or the dorm faculty; say that they're cracking down especially hard lately. I'll even say that I have a sports event tomorrow and need to make sure I'm on my A-game.

Unfortunately, mistakes sometimes do happen.

IF YOU MAKE A MISTAKE

It was the last weekend of my sophomore year, the Saturday before exams. The week had been a long one, spent mostly in the library, while temperatures outside rose and the sky emptied itself of clouds. The result was a warm June night with a starlit sky, and 800 kids nearly at their breaking point.

That night, I went bridge-jumping with some friends, and then joined a game of Marco Polo in the river. When I finally got out, my phone screen was illuminated with three texts from my friend Amanda.

8:30 p.m. – Heyyy! I'm with Betsy and Ariana. I'll be back on campus for the dance.

9:00 p.m. – Soo wasted right now

9:15 p.m. – OMG! Dean Smith is here with a Breathalyzer. He's going to catch me. Helppp!!!

I glanced at my phone again to check the time. It now read 9:18 p.m. I tapped the "Call" button. Amanda picked up, and I told her I thought I should "NDI" her. She instantly agreed.

My school offers a Non-Disciplinary Intervention (NDI) program. It is a nondisciplinary response to a drug- or alcohol-related issue. By NDI-ing Amanda, I alerted the school counselors that Amanda had made a poor decision. Instead of a disciplinary charge, Amanda participated in one term of regular counseling sessions on decision making.

Many other schools have programs similar to NDI. Another boarding school I know, for example, provides a nondisciplinary option called Crisis. Usually, information about these programs can be found in the school rulebook or by talking to your house counselor or other trusted adult.

Unfortunately, I was not able to NDI Betsy and Ariana. Both were intoxicated that night, and both received major disciplinary cases.

Behavior that deviates from my school's expected standards warrants an Infraction Committee Case (ICC). When Betsy and Ariana drank, they committed a major infraction. At most schools, major infractions include drinking, smoking, hazing, bullying, plagiarism, cheating, and leaving the campus without permission. Consult your school's rulebook for its specific descriptions and definitions of infractions.

ICC's are held one evening each week at my school. During a case, a committee hears the facts of the situation. The student charged gives a statement, then both a faculty member and a peer read a character statement. The committee then deliberates, and a verdict is delivered by the end of the night.

Betsy was required to leave the school, while Ariana was put on restrictions with probation, meaning any other minor infraction would result in expulsion. Because Amanda and I sought help, she avoided disciplinary action and set herself on an ultimately healthier path.

This was one of many instances where seeking help is the most important thing you can do. For the first half of my freshman year, I was too shy to seek help from adults. I worried that asking for help was babyish and immature, an admission of some sort of weakness. But my attitude changed sometime in the middle of Winter Term, when one of my best friends, Aaron, was hazed.

STAY SAFE

It was a Tuesday night, and the boys in Green Dorm were crowded into their common room.

"All right, boys. This is it. This Friday night will be the Freshmen Pillow Fight," one of the seniors said. He continued to explain that every year, each freshman is zipped into a laundry bag and thrown off one of the loft beds. The goal was to hit the couch on the other side of the room, but occasionally, freshmen landed on the floor instead of the couch.

Aaron dreaded Friday all week.

Finally, at the dining hall on Thursday night, Aaron told our dinner table about the impending "pillow fight." He said that he had already asked the upperclassmen to cancel it, but they had been adamant.

"I just don't know what to do," Aaron said. "It seems kind of like a tradition, and I don't want to ruin anything. But I really don't want a broken arm or something."

We all just looked at each other, then down at the dishes, pushing food around our plates with our forks. The frosty silence at our table was palpable.

"You could talk to Mr. Jones. He's pretty chill," I suggested, still pushing rice around my plate.

"Yeah, Mr. Jones is cool. I think that maybe I should. I feel bad, but… " Aaron trailed off and shrugged.

Aaron came to dinner the next night, visibly relaxed.

"How'd it go?" I asked.

He smiled. "Really, really well."

He explained that once he went to Mr. Jones, the house counselor in his dorm, other freshmen came forward and expressed similar concerns.

Of course, some of the ringleaders were angry. Aaron and his friends dealt with an occasional cold shoulder and snide comment on the pathway for the next few days. But, looking back, Aaron knew that the benefits vastly outweighed the negatives. Ninety-five percent of their dormmates hadn't cared, and perhaps more importantly, Aaron found a faculty member he could trust.

Unfortunately, the bullies who planned to haze Aaron exist everywhere, not just at my school. Living with bullies, as opposed to merely going to school with them, can magnify typical high school bullying problems. To keep dorm life as stress-free as possible, try not to engage with them. Handle them with politeness, but keep your distance.

At my school, hazing, bullying, and substance abuse are all addressed through a required health course, taken freshman year. Throughout the year, the school also has a series of assemblies with speakers who address similar issues. Dorms gather regularly for meetings to discuss these topics, too.

Cheating and plagiarism are two other common infractions at boarding school, and most schools take them very seriously. A friend of my older sister, while writing a history paper, once forgot to cite a source. Her teacher noticed, and accused her of plagiarism. Luckily, she only received minor punishment because she didn't plagiarize purposefully, but from then on I've been very careful to give credit where credit is due. I've learned that the best policy when writing a paper is, "When in doubt, cite it out."

But the bottom line is this: boarding school is an incredible experience. As with anything, though, the good comes with some bad. Navigating the ins and outs of boarding school is almost a rite of passage. So, my advice?

- Be confident and relax.
- Hang out with people who make you feel comfortable.
- Stand up to bullies. Being a bystander is almost as bad as being a bully.
- Make decisions that you (and your parents) can be proud of. If it doesn't feel right to you, it probably isn't right. Go with your gut.
- Using drugs or alcohol is illegal. Why put your high school record and career at risk by breaking the law or for a quick, fleeting night of debauchery? It's just not worth it.
- Know your school's rules and the punishments for infractions. You don't want to end up with a disciplinary case for doing something you didn't know was prohibited.
- Above all, enjoy boarding school. Make good decisions, and your four years at boarding school could be some of the best in your life.

ABOUT "JANE DOE"

I am a third-year student in boarding school. I enjoy running cross-country in the fall, swimming in the winter, and running track in the spring. I am also very involved with the Best Buddies program and participate in a few other clubs, including an environmental awareness club and a peer-tutoring program. My favorite part of boarding school? The people. And, of course, the dining hall's French fries.

CHAPTER 22
Day Students: Finding Your Place

by Ellen Sukharevsky
Milton Academy—Milton, Massachusetts—Class of 2013
Hometown: Boston, Massachusetts

A Note from Justin: A "day student" can mean different things at different boarding schools. Some schools may assign day students roommates and a dorm room where they can sleep on nights that they will be on campus very late. Other "day students" actually board during the week and go home on weekends. This chapter, however, focuses on the "pure" day-student experience: a student who lives exclusively at home and comes to the school campus for classes and extracurricular activities.

R ING! RING! My iPhone alarm startles me awake. I roll over, look at the time, and groan. It's about 6 a.m. Maybe I could just sleep for 5 more minutes—it won't hurt, right? But those extra 5 minutes in the morning can make all the difference when it comes to beating traffic on the way to school…

I'm a day student at Milton Academy, which sets me apart from about 50 percent of the school community. (In most boarding schools, day students compose about 10 to 20 percent of the school population.) Frankly, being a day student at a boarding school isn't that bad. Many people give me sympathetic looks when I say I don't live on campus, and most boarders like to boast a bit about their status, listing dozens of benefits to being a boarder (sleeping in on weekends, not having to deal with transportation issues, having more independence, and so on). But at the end of the day, who gets to go home to a nice fluffy bed, a home-cooked meal, and the family? That's right, day students.

Let me start off by describing a typical day in the life of a day student. I wake up early (around 6 a.m. for me, but it really depends on how close to school you live), eat breakfast, brush teeth, get dressed/put on makeup (yes, as a girl, it takes me longer to get ready in the morning, but I've perfected an efficient beauty routine). No, I can't just step out of the house in pajamas and change later (like many boarders do), because I live with my parents and still have to respect their standards of living and dressing. I once asked my boarder friend Allison what she thought was the biggest difference between day students and boarders, and she responded, "I get to set my own boundaries. No parents, no rules about clothing or food or cleanliness; I am independent and get to decide for myself how I live." She's right—I have to pass the "parent-approval test" before I walk out the door and go to school. Of course, there isn't really a test and I'm mostly joking; but the fact is that parents play a bigger role in a day student's life, and everything we do is still scrutinized by them.

So, back to the typical day. After the long drive to school, my day is pretty much the same as a boarder's. One difference, though, is that I can't go back to a dorm to change clothes or get books for different classes, so I have to be much more prepared every day. Instead of the cute purses and knapsacks that boarders use, I lug all of my textbooks around in a heavy-duty backpack. The good news, though, is that most campuses have a day-student lounge where students can have a locker or cubby area to store books and extra items for the day. That way, my backpack never gets *too* heavy. After my sports or classes end, I am just a car ride away from home, food, and my extremely comfortable bed.

In addition to the commute and home life, day students sometimes don't get the chance to develop as strong a community as boarders do, since we go home every evening. At Milton, boarders are all required to eat with their dorm community at a sit-down dinner three days a week, and there are all kinds of fun traditions and activities, like their big fancy Christmas dinner. They're more closely knit than the day-student community, with other traditions such as caroling (where the guys and girls in each dorm serenade each other) or activities like dorm bowling and dodge ball tournaments. Day students can sometimes feel left out and a bit jealous of these traditions. I have also heard many day students complain that it's easier for boarders to make friends because they live together and are able to socialize more, while day students aren't as involved in the school community.

But don't worry—being a day student shouldn't stop you from making friends and being part of the school community. You should definitely make an effort to join in campus activities and interact with a wide range of students because it will help you become a part of the community. Day students and boarders can be friends, too! Don't be afraid to reach out to boarders and invite them to your house for a home-cooked meal or to spend the night on a long weekend when they might not be able to go home because their families live too far away. You can also invite them to join you and your family for a weekend activity if your school allows it. Believe me, boarders are delighted to spend some time away from the dorm! And this process works the other way around, too; you can take advantage of the fact that you have boarder friends and spend time in their dorm, use their kitchen, leave your stuff in their room, etc. My best friend at Milton is a boarder, and I always hang out in her room, dump my heavy backpack there, change clothes for sports, and eat with her at dorm dinners. People in her dorm refer to me as an honorary member of their group. At Milton, day students in general are often called "honorary boarders," because the boarding community is very welcoming and connected to the day-student community.

It's up to you to meet people; I can't give you a step-by-step guide to making friends. I can, however, suggest a few pointers on making the most of your time as a day student. Here are my suggestions for building a more successful and integrated day-student experience at a boarding school:

Talk to people.
Try to interact with people involved in the same things as you.

Don't get sucked too deeply into the routine of school, home, work, sleep, school.
It's easy to walk around on autopilot and spend all your days navigating the hallways like a zombie, but try not to do that. Change up your routine, go to clubs, stay on campus late every once in a while, and participate in activities or sports. This will expose you to the school community and can be a great way to meet people.

Participate in activities.
I cannot emphasize enough the importance of clubs and extracurriculars in a day student's high school experience. As a day student, it's easy to just go home right after classes, but you'll have a better time in school if you have some fun, try new things, and expand your interests.

Be respectful of your classmates, and though it sounds obvious, try not to say anything mean.
Be considerate of others anywhere and anytime that you are with a group of friends. Steer clear of gossip about boarders or day students. Remember that the conversations you have about others will likely get back to them.

Stay over one night in a dorm.
This is a great way to experience more of life at your school, especially if there is a late-night weekend activity and you don't feel like going home right afterwards.

Approach people in the student center or at lunch and just have a conversation with them.
Don't be afraid to mingle with boarders or classmates you don't know. It may surprise you how open people are, and you could even make some more friends. Try to talk to someone older than you; they give great advice and are just really cool!

Be sensitive and kind to boarders and see how you can support them.
Having a friend with parents nearby can be a huge plus for boarders, giving them a surrogate family off campus. See if there are ways you can help, whether it's picking something up for them off campus (groceries, supplies, or even a prescription), driving them to a haircut, or bringing them chicken soup if they feel sick. This can mean a lot to a boarder whose parents are far away. Imagine life in the shoes of your boarding friends, and find ways to be helpful and loyal.

Being a day student can be a great experience! Here are my Top 10 benefits to being a day student at a boarding school:

1. Home-cooked meals.

2. No dorm sign-ins and sign-outs.

3. Your mom will take care of you when you're sick.

4. No need to do your own laundry.

5. You can go off campus more freely.

6. No strict curfew or lights-out policies.

7. Unlimited Internet access (many schools block access after a certain time to help enforce lights-out policies).

8. No need to rely on Amazon or other shipping services for all of life's essentials.

9. Your parents can come to see your sporting events, theatrical or dance programs, or awards ceremonies. And you will always be able to celebrate your birthday with your family.

10. Once you reach the right age, you can drive yourself to school (assuming there is an available car).

Even though you're not a boarder, you can still have a positive boarding school experience. I have grown to love my day-student life, and day students can have a great time at boarding school if they are social, kind, and not afraid to reach out to people.

ABOUT ELLEN SUKHAREVSKY

I graduated cum laude from Milton Academy in 2013 and attend Brown University. I am interested in medical science and genetics and plan on concentrating in health and human biology. I am also fluent in four languages (Russian, French, Spanish, and English) and enjoy writing. At Milton, I was the founder of the French newspaper *Mille Tonnes* as well as the student research group. I wrote for *The Milton Paper* and was the head of the French club for two years. I participated in cross-country, volleyball, and tennis. At Brown, I have continued writing, am exploring the open curriculum, and joined the Division One crew team.

CHAPTER 23
International Students: Transitioning to a New Country and Culture

by Shihao Hu
South Kent School—South Kent, Connecticut—Class of 2014
Hometown: Hangzhou, China

__A Note from Justin:__ This chapter focuses on the experience of a student from China. All prospective international students should be sure to check with their respective governmental agencies for specific details regarding student visas, certificates, or authorizations needed to study abroad. The international admission officer from your prospective schools should also be able to advise you on these matters.

As I reflect upon my life as a student, applying to boarding schools stands out as perhaps the most important and challenging experience I have ever undertaken. My experience is not unusual; hundreds of thousands of Chinese students seek out an American education. From afar, boarding school looks like the quickest and easiest route to success, but for many international students, simply applying is an incredibly rigorous process in and of itself. However, I do not regret my choice to apply, because so far, boarding school has been an invaluable part of my life. This chapter provides some personal anecdotes as well as suggestions for aspiring international students who seek to study in the United States and achieve their dreams.

FINDING A CONSULTANT

It was the June before my freshman year of high school, and I was quite happy to be matriculating to the Xuejun High School, a prestigious Chinese day school known for the high scores its students earn on the College Entrance Exam of China. But one summer night, my father asked me whether I wanted to study at a U.S. boarding school. In truth, I had considered this possibility for a long time, since Tom, one of my best friends, decided to attend high school abroad. As a smart, talented, and kind person, Tom was one of my role models. For this reason, his choice carried a lot of weight. I've also had a lifelong admiration of the ideals of freedom and liberty in the United States, reinforced by my inherent curiosity about exotic cultures. So when my dad proposed the idea, I said, "Yes, I'd love to apply!"

The very next day, my father and I went to Zhejiang Shinyway International, a consulting firm, and signed a contract. Shinyway would take care of my application process, including training for the required tests, finding a "proper" high school, composing my résumé, and helping me obtain an F-1 visa. Shinyway also provided a summer camp for SSAT® and TOEFL® training and promised to get me into a top-100 American high school (based on the average SAT score of graduating students). In return for these services, my family had to pay $15,000. Most of my friends who wanted to study abroad also used a consulting firm like this one.

TEST PREPARATION

The test-prep course was held over the summer at a middle school campus. The course was two-months long—one month devoted to the SSAT, another to the TOEFL. Each day, there were two or three 2-hour classes in speaking, reading, writing, vocabulary, and math. The rest of the day was devoted to individual review. Like the school year, we had class five days a week, so the weekends were spent sorting through school options and preparing for interviews. For many international students, standardized test preparation is the highest priority because of a misconception that a perfect score on the SSAT or TOEFL guarantees acceptance to the most prestigious schools. In reality, you shouldn't worry if you don't do as well as someone else on these tests. While standardized test scores are certainly important, the other parts of an application are just as significant.

THE APPLICATION

Soon fall came. I went to Xuejun High School for my freshman year. It was tiring to both study for my classes and work on my applications to American schools. Once or twice a month, I would meet with my consultant to continue my search for schools. Based on my interests, my preferred locations, campus life, school sports teams, and most importantly, my chances of being accepted, he picked eight schools for me. Shinyway then helped reorganize my materials, compose a résumé, and put me in touch with the schools' admission officers.

My consultant also revised my essays for each school to correct the grammar and embellish the writing. Later, when I talked with my American teachers, I learned that they strongly disapproved of having my consultant revise my essays. For you, I would recommend that you allow your own voice to shine through in your essays, even if your grammar and choice of words isn't entirely perfect. Admission staff members want to get a sample of you and your personality, and having someone else help write your essays can be detrimental.

It's a good idea for international students to pay attention and demonstrate effort when putting together their résumés. For example, if you have a particular athletic, musical, or other talent, ask if you may submit a short video sample. American schools do not look for formulaic transcripts or monotonous essays; instead, they want a vivid image of you. You need to provide enough material for them so that they can get to know you better.

THE INTERVIEWS

I was relieved when I had finally submitted all eight applications (transcripts, test scores, letters of recommendation, essays, and résumés) to the schools. But that was just the first step. I still needed to train for the interviews. I watched American TV shows like *The Big Bang Theory* and went to tourist areas in Shanghai to talk to English-speaking foreigners in order to practice my conversational English. I would recommend that you do something like this, too, so you are able to feel comfortable talking to an admission officer. My consultant also conducted practice interviews to test and improve my ability to hold a conversation in English. In addition, I visited the school websites to search for information, and I learned the school mottos and thought of questions about each institution so I could impress the interviewers and anticipate what type of questions they would ask me.

Sometimes, I had the opportunity to attend high school fairs held in Shanghai, where representatives from American boarding schools would speak with thousands of eager Chinese students. There, I met admission officers from three schools and had interviews with them. By chatting with them in person, I was able to make a better impression than I could have done via Skype. If you have the chance to interview in person, do it.

For international students especially, the interview is the most important way for admission officers to learn who you are as a person. If you stand out in the interviewer's assessment as being different, special, and interesting, then you have succeeded. Don't try to address some broad topic like global warming or international poverty. Dreaming big is good, but being yourself is better. If you have a Skype interview, be sure to check your Internet connection and volume before you begin. A Skype interview is better than a phone call because with Skype, an admission officer can put a face to a name. If possible, though, find a time to travel to the schools with your parents (if this is within your budget) or attend local fairs to talk to the admission officers face-to-face.

THE RESULT

Waiting for decision day is always stressful. During the time between the day that I submitted my applications to the day that the schools made their decisions, I started to worry: Will they accept me? Can I get into these schools? What if every school rejects me? More than once I woke up at 4 a.m., sweating due to an anxiety-induced nightmare. On decision day, I kept refreshing my e-mail inbox to see the results. Every time I clicked on an e-mail with a bold-letter title, my heart sank a little: four rejections, three waitlists, and only one acceptance. I was so jealous when I heard friends complain how hard it was for them to pick just one school. On the other hand, I was thrilled to have been accepted by South Kent and to know I would be going to a U.S. boarding school. If you do get rejected or waitlisted, though, don't despair! Inquire about openings on the waitlist; you still might have a chance.

LEAVING HOME

In June, after everything settled down, I started to prepare to leave. Over the summer, some of my friends who were going to attend an American school took an English course to further improve their speaking skills, while others chose to attend summer school in the United States to get exposed to American culture earlier. But I chose to spend time with my family and visit other friends and relatives. If you are close to your family, you might consider spending your summers savoring your time together.

When it was time to pack, I followed the instructions sent by my school and brought essentials like clothes and bedding. I also packed a lot of books and school supplies. That said, almost everything you need can be found once you're here, online (Amazon), at local stores (Walmart, CVS, etc.), or your school's student store.

NEW SCHOOL, NEW LIFE

I still remember the heavy rain pouring down when I arrived at JFK Airport in New York City. Staring at the gray sky I thought, "Well, my life will be as gloomy as the weather." But as it turned out, my nostalgia and wistful pessimism was unfounded. At school, I was assigned an advisor who helped me with academic, athletic, and personal needs. I also was matched with a local family who hosted me during long weekends and breaks when I could not go home.

There were certainly some aspects of boarding school life that I found difficult to deal with. The first was my listening and speaking ability. During the first three months, I could hardly follow the conversations of my classmates and teachers. However, it is acceptable for international students to have these comprehension issues in the beginning. As long as you are courageous enough to speak with Americans, they will be kind in return. Be optimistic, confident, and humorous, and don't be afraid to step out of your comfort zone. I have noticed that many international students, especially Asians, like to hang out only with others from their home country, and speak exclusively in their native language with them. This is a huge problem that will definitely not help you fit into your new environment. In order to improve your English-speaking skills and acclimate socially, you have to make some American friends and try to be outgoing.

If you stumble in your academic journey, ask an older student for help. The summer before I left China, I sent a couple of e-mails to my prefect, and he turned out to be quite helpful. I recently became a prefect myself. This summer I have exchanged e-mails with incoming students from China, and I've even met some of them personally to explain how to adjust to boarding school life. Trust me, older students—especially prefects or other international students—want to help. They were once in your shoes, and they had similar problems or difficulties.

TIPS FOR INTERNATIONAL STUDENTS

It isn't easy for students to study abroad. We face conflicts in language, culture, and customs. I hope what I have shared will help you in your boarding school application process. Here are my suggested tips for international students considering a boarding school education in the United States:

- Find a consultant only if your family is able to do so financially. Brokerage fees can range from $10,000 to $20,000, so this is certainly an expensive investment.

- If you cannot afford a consultant, seek help from your local school guidance counselor or the international admission officer affiliated with the schools to which you are applying.

- Work hard to get good SSAT and TOEFL scores. Higher scores do help you qualify as a candidate to a wider range of schools.

- Test scores, though, just signal that you are diligent and test well, like thousands of others. Show admission officers that you are special, different, and outstanding, and that you will contribute positively to their school.

- Don't be shy about sending admission officers e-mails to ask specific questions or arrange interviews.

- Even though you are an international student, paying a visit to a prospective school is definitely worth it. Speaking confidently and fluently with admission officers in person allows them to get to know you better.

- If offered, a nonstop flight is always a good option when traveling to and from school. You have enough on your plate, so why not make your life a little easier?

ABOUT SHIHAO HU

I am a Chinese student enrolled at South Kent School in Connecticut. I transferred from China during my sophomore year. Currently, I am a school prefect primarily responsible for taking care of international students' affairs. Throughout my time at South Kent, I have participated in the Visions program in Ghana to build an orphanage, the Bishops' 5K for Kids road race, an exchange program with the Czech Republic, and the Harvard-MIT Mathematics Tournament. I also play soccer and golf and run cross-country. In addition, I am a writer for the school newspaper, *The Pigtail*. In my free time, I enjoy reading and writing.

CHAPTER 24
Entering Boarding School after Freshman Year: Starting "Off Sequence"

by Evan Lee
The Lawrenceville School—Lawrence Township, NJ—Class of 2015
Hometown: Greenwich, Connecticut

A Note from Justin: Usually the term "upperclassman" refers to a junior or senior student. But for the purposes of this chapter, "upperclassman" will be defined as any non-freshman student—meaning a sophomore, junior, senior, or postgraduate (PG).

Congratulations! If you are reading this section, then you're a rising upperclassman who decided to make the jump to boarding school after freshman year. Though boarding school is a wonderful experience, the drive to apply must come entirely from you—even more so if you are entering "off sequence," at a time other than your freshman year. If your parents are forcing you to apply, or if you view boarding school as a way to have fun and goof off, you need to give more thought as to whether you truly want to attend. Switching to boarding school as a new upperclassman can be disruptive to your high school career, and you need to be prepared to handle the challenges of assimilating to a new environment. Your classmates who started boarding school earlier have a social and perhaps academic advantage. They have already had an entire year or more to acclimate and learn from their mistakes. To succeed as a transfer student, you need the drive, passion, excitement, and maturity to get off to a good start right away. That said, you needn't be intimidated—boarding school is one of the best choices I ever made. If you feel that boarding school is a good choice, and you are not afraid of hard work, I urge you to apply.

I wanted to write this chapter because when I applied to boarding school for entry into tenth grade, I couldn't find very much advice for kids entering as upperclassmen. I thought that this subject needed to be addressed, since some schools admit over a third of their graduating classes after freshman year. Having just completed my first year at The Lawrenceville School, I have some tips to help you make a smooth transition into boarding school.

SOCIAL TIPS FOR A TRANSFER STUDENT

- **Key Advice: This is not the time to be shy.** You may need to venture outside your comfort zone and be very outgoing in order to make new friends. Remember, the students in class you will be joining have bonded throughout the previous year(s) and may not be so eager to meet new students as they were during their freshman year. Though there will be some activities to get to know other new students, there will probably not be mixers or icebreaker activities with your returning classmates. So what should you do to integrate yourself socially?

- **Introduce yourself and say hello to as many people as possible during the first couple of months of school.** I learned this when I started Lawrenceville as a new sophomore. Since you are new, you have the perfect excuse to approach other students and ask them their name. Even if after a few weeks you know who someone is but have never talked to them, just go up and introduce yourself. It's very important to make contact and connections with classmates early in the year. Besides, in the beginning of the school year, no one will judge you. Yes, transfer students need to be bolder in order to hold their own in their school's social circles.

- **Join clubs.** I can't stress this enough. Even if you only have a slight interest in a club, just sign up and give it a try. You will end up paring down the number of clubs in which you want to get fully involved, but you will also meet many people in the process. At Lawrenceville, and most boarding schools, a club fair is held at the beginning of each year. This is a great time to sign up. Clubs allow you to network and meet people who share your interests. Who knows, you may discover a new passion as well!

- **Sports teams or other group activities are an equally good way to make friends.** If you spend a couple of hours every day with a group of guys or girls, you're bound to make a few close friends. During the fall term, it's especially important to have teammates (at any level of any sport) with whom to build camaraderie. If you're not into sports, trying things like dance or the school musical are also great ways to mesh with the school community.

- **If there are any new student orientation events at all, go to them!** For example, the summer before I started tenth grade, I got an e-mail about a "new sophomore camping trip." Initially, I wasn't sure that I wanted to cut my vacation short and go to school five days early to hike 20 miles on the Appalachian Trail. But I decided to go, and it ended up being one of the best choices I made. Since everyone else on that trip was a new sophomore, I had a core group of friends going into the first day of school. It made adjusting to Lawrenceville easier and got rid of a potentially awkward first week where I didn't know anybody. While most of the camping crew ended up drifting apart, I am still extremely close to a couple of those students. So take advantage of any and all new-student orientations!

DORM SURVIVAL

- **In the dorm, reach out to people who come from your hometown or state.** Geographic proximity can provide an automatic connection, and these are fairly easy relationships to forge. You might even become close enough to carpool or book the same flight when returning home during breaks. In addition, it's really important to get close to the kids on your floor or hall since you will run into them often. When you see them in the morning, at night, in the common room, or even in the bathroom, be sure to be friendly and strike up a conversation (for example, "Hey, cool flip-flops!").

- **Be aware that the kids in your dorm might already be close friends who have requested to live together.** Don't worry, though—boarding school kids are generally really nice and will be open to new friendships. Just be authentic, engaging, and open-minded. Stay true to yourself, and be sure of your values.

- **Go to every event your dorm holds during the fall term.** You might notice some kids who skip a meeting or activity or two. Don't do that! Your best chances of bonding with anyone at the school will be with your dormmates. If you don't capitalize on opportunities to hang out with them, you might miss the opportunity to find a new good friend.

STAY HEALTHY

- **Go to sleep as early as you can!** Minimize late-night distractions like texting and the Internet. Everyone else in the dorm already knows his or her threshold for sleep deprivation. If you try to match what your dormmates do, you're going to collapse in your first term.

- **Eat breakfast every morning.** When I started at Lawrenceville, I initially skipped breakfast in order to get extra sleep (see advice above). However, I learned very quickly that without food in my stomach I would run out of mental and physical steam by late morning. You definitely need to eat something in the morning—even if it's just a bagel, a nutrition bar, or a protein shake. You can buy nonperishable food items at the local drugstore, student store, or deli. You can even order nonperishable food from Amazon! Of course, it's always best to get up early enough to have breakfast in the cafeteria whenever possible.

BE SMART ABOUT ACADEMICS

- **Try to balance your academic and social life.** Fall term is when most new sophomores struggle academically, as they are adjusting to the rigor of boarding school. While it's smart and healthy to make friends, don't get overly sidetracked by social temptation in the beginning. It is important to remember that even while you focus on integrating socially, staying on top of your academics should be your top priority.

- **Study and work hard.** At Lawrenceville, freshmen are given "pass or fail" grades for their entire first term as they get used to boarding school. Similarly, other boarding schools may make it easier on freshmen to help keep the first year a transitional one. Unfortunately, as a new upperclassman, you're not going to get this luxury, since teachers will have the same expectations for you as they do for everyone else. You really have to hit the books and get cracking!

- **Go into your first term well-organized, with binders for each specific class.** You can ask your dormmates for specific tips on studying, homework, and organization that apply to your own school. Once you get past fall term, the academic transition gets much easier!

- **Take another look at your schedule and graduation requirements.** When you enter as an upperclassman, you may not know which classes are better or worse from a student perspective. Returning students have insider knowledge that they've heard through the grapevine or learned firsthand. Once you arrive on campus, ask other students about your schedule and, if you need to, switch classes. For example, I originally signed up for music theory to fulfill my arts requirement, but then I learned it was an extremely time-consuming class. Since I also enjoy art and photography, I switched to a lighter class called Art Foundation so I could focus more on my core courses.

- **Find the course load that's right for you.** At your previous high school, you may have been a big fish in a smaller pond, so you took the most rigorous classes available. But at boarding school, you might discover that quite a few kids in your grade are taking more advanced classes than you are. This is especially hard to handle for someone who started his or her high school career at the very top of the class. That's what happened to me. While it bothered me initially, I quickly realized that I just needed to do my best and take the toughest classes that I could handle without worrying what my peers were doing. If you have questions about your schedule or classes, talk to your advisor or find a teacher who can answer your questions and help you.

- **Speak up!** This is really important. You need to actively seek out and communicate with your teachers. While it may have been enough to see your teachers only during class time at your previous school, it's important to develop relationships with your teachers at boarding school. Most of them live on campus and are going to be available much more than those at a typical day school. Also, cultivate a good relationship with your advisor and house counselor. They are there to support you. My advice is to find at least one adult whom you trust and respect. That person can be a teacher, coach, or any other faculty member or administrator. During my first term, I had an immediate connection with my English teacher, Mr. Kane. Now I see him during consultation periods, and we have great discussions about everything from literature to the latest sports news. Sometimes we continue our conversations while walking to the cafeteria together. Having a comfortable relationship with a teacher definitely helped make my transition to boarding school a lot more enjoyable.

THE POSTGRADUATE (PG) YEAR

The PG year is a mystery to many people who aren't familiar with boarding schools, but here's what I know. Sometimes, a student who has already graduated from high school will attend a boarding school for their "thirteenth" year. In most cases, these students are athletes who want to hone their skills for another year before applying to college or getting recruited. However, a student may also choose to do a PG year to mature a bit before college. Since most PG students are athletes or those who have talents in a specific area, they will usually find their niche within their team or specific group or activity. While the PG program may seem unconventional, it is definitely an accepted part of boarding school life. All of my advice for students entering out of sequence applies to PGs as well.

CLOSING THOUGHTS

It might sound simplistic, but just enjoy yourself. You may have heard the saying that at boarding school, there is time to sleep, socialize, or study—and you can only choose two. However, if you get your priorities in order, work efficiently, and have a little self control, you can definitely find time for all three and enjoy your high school career.

ABOUT EVAN LEE

I was exposed to the idea of boarding school after spending my seventh grade summer at a Johns Hopkins Center for Talented Youth (CTY) program. Not only did I meet students who attended boarding school, but I became friends with smart and passionate kids from all over the world. This experience made me realize that I wanted to be in this kind of environment 24/7. One glitch: my parents liked having me at home, and boarding school was nowhere on their radar. They did not let me apply for freshman year. But I didn't give up, and I laid out my case again in the fall of ninth grade. This time, my parents allowed me to apply. I'll admit that as fall approached, I started to feel a little nervous, as there were many unknowns ahead. However, I can honestly say that taking that risk and leaving my safe and comfortable path has paid off. I had my best year ever! My clubs, interests, and positions at Lawrenceville include these: varsity indoor and outdoor track teams (pole vault), executive photo editor of Lawrenceville's yearbook (the *Olla Pod*), president of the Innocence Project Club and activist for Fernando Bermudez (innocent man exonerated after eighteen years of incarceration), creator of Aerobeats.com (a music blog), treasurer of Griswold House, ropes course instructor, saxophone player in the jazz band, and member of the Fellowship of Christian Athletes.

CHAPTER 25
Summer Opportunities: Making Good Use of Your Down Time

by Wendy Huang
St. Paul's School—Concord, New Hampshire—Class of 2014
Hometown: Acton, Massachusetts

It's 4 a.m. when we step outside of the dorm. The night air—or, more accurately, the early morning air—is comfortable. Philadelphia's summers are terribly humid, but for the first time, my shirt doesn't cling to my back. Walking next to me is a small group of friends. We've only known each other for about four weeks, but we feel as though we've been lifelong friends. It's the last morning before everyone leaves the University of Pennsylvania's Wharton School's precollege business program, Leadership in the Business World (LBW). Walking around the school's quadrangle, we begin to reminisce. It's bittersweet. Looking forward, we doubt that we'll all cross paths again. But looking back, the 60 of us who were accepted into the LBW program agree that it enabled us to do remarkable things.

In a mere four weeks, we visited several multibillion-dollar companies, wrote business proposals and pitched them to venture capitalists, attended lectures from some of Wharton's most esteemed professors, and made friends with some wonderfully witty and smart people. As high school students, each of us realizes how fortunate we are. Exclusive information sessions with Bergdorf Goodman, Morgan Stanley, Google, Tesla, Deloitte Consulting, and American Express (to name a few) are not usually accessible to high school students. At first, it's hard to even imagine why these companies would take time out of their schedules for us. But I've learned from LBW that smart investors look for opportunities of low risk. These companies and their senior officials are investing in their futures by talking to us, because they expect us to be exceptional. After meeting everyone at LBW, I can honestly say that these companies have made a smart investment.

With an acceptance rate that rivals many top universities, LBW employs a fairly rigorous and holistic application process to find those 60 accepted individuals. And LBW chooses well. Within the program, I met students who started their own nonprofit organizations, students who have more than $100,000 invested in the stock market, and students who aspire to be the next great entrepreneur.

Of course, I don't mean to insinuate that anyone who doesn't get to attend LBW is destined for a bleak future and that everyone who does attend is going to be great. To be honest, before LBW, I had no clear idea of exactly what "business" meant. I simply knew I was interested, and that was perfectly fine! There are hundreds of summer programs out there, not just LBW, and they all inspire students to be their best. And this is where my first piece of advice for boarding school students looking for summer opportunities comes in.

START EXPLORING

Seriously, choose a subject and explore. Junior year and fall-term senior year are arguably the two most important times in a high school student's career. But between these two stressful stretches lies the equally important summer months. That summer is a great time to supplement your education. Whether you take part in community service, athletic camps, or leadership experiences, as long as you get out of the house there isn't much that can go wrong. I've spent countless summers in front of my TV or computer monitor, and it wasn't ever really worth it. By getting up off the couch and attending LBW and having an internship before that, I think that I learned more in one summer than I have ever learned in all my previous summers combined. So, don't be like me—start exploring early! I have a friend who went to a medical program before LBW simply because he thought he would be interested. He had a wonderful time at the medical program and learned that it wasn't for him. As a high school student, this is a lucky lesson to learn. By putting yourself out there, you can find out firsthand what you really are passionate about—or not. Many of us heading into college don't really know what we want. It's always easier to have a major choose you rather than you choose a major. By attending summer programs to figure out what fields interest you, your future major might appear.

Thus, exploring is the best thing you can do in the summer. One friend of mine ventured into the city with her camera, and simply by leaving home, she met unique people and delved into the world of photojournalism. Another friend reached out to several university professors at his local college and offered his support as a research assistant. Whether through a structured program or not, exploring will inevitably lead you to interesting people. Although the academic portion of LBW was amazing, it was the people who really made the program. The same can be said for almost everything in life; the people are truly the most important aspect of any business, school, or environment.

SEEK ENRICHMENT

My second piece of advice is to seek enrichment. There comes a point when taking six weeks of BC Calculus just to be ahead of your peers may not be the best use of your time. Of course, if you have to take a summer course as a prerequisite or you really do need that extra work, that's fine. But if you ever have a choice between a credit course and a noncredit course, the noncredit course is probably going to be better and more fulfilling. With a noncredit course like LBW, you really receive enrichment without the fear of a bad grade. At school—and this is especially applicable to boarding schools—we've already learned how to study. We know what it's like to put hours into a paper, cram the night before a test, and live with a get-it-done mentality. The summer is a wonderful time to truly learn for learning's sake.

High school students will sometimes grumble about the classes they have to take. After all, advanced mathematics isn't always applicable to everyday life. So why spend your summer doing something to boost your transcript?

GET STARTED EARLY

Honestly, this may be the most important piece of advice I can give you. You can't go exploring or choose an enriching program if your options aren't clear to you. Much like boarding school or college admissions, serious summer programs begin their selection process early. In the fall, summer has just passed and you couldn't care less about what you're going to do the next summer. However, some of the best programs have applications due in early January. Once you factor in time for writing an essay and getting teacher recommendations, you'll realize that the application process needs to start in December at the latest. For programs where the application is due later, your December–January holiday break offers a wonderful block of time to complete this process.

In my junior year, I didn't know that the process started so early, and I missed the deadlines for some really interesting programs. In fact, I almost missed the LBW deadline. Looking back, I'm so grateful for my friend who told me about the program just a few weeks before the application was due. I had an incredible time at LBW, and I cannot believe I came so close to missing this amazing opportunity. The longer you wait to research, the greater the chance that you will miss that one special program.

That being said, here are some programs I've heard great things about and had on my list last winter. Aside from my obvious love for Wharton's LBW program, I was seriously considering Yale's Young Ivy Scholars Program in Grand Strategy. Yale also has a program called PLE (Politics, Law, and Economics) that seemed interesting to me, too. From what I've heard from friends, those two programs include more academics than LBW, but they're still incredibly enriching. The Telluride Association Summer Program (TASP) is completely free and covers many aspects of the humanities. It is also incredibly prestigious, and there is a rigorous application process. Similarly, the Center for Excellence in Education offers its Research Science Institute (RSI) program. RSI is focused on science and technology research, and, like TASP, it is also free of charge.

Those are just a few of the many programs that may be available to you. My knowledge of summer programs is limited, so don't be afraid to reach out to the other resources available to you. In today's age, the Internet may be the most valuable tool to have. Doing a general Google search is a good way to start, but there are also Internet databases aimed at helping students find internships and language exchanges. For example, Julian Krinsky Camps and Programs does a wonderful job of matching students and their passions to potential internships. Also, internships.com has a huge selection of internships in many different fields. Aside from the Internet, you can also visit your school's college counseling or summer opportunities department, or you can talk to your teachers and advisor. Many adults on your boarding school campus have extensive knowledge about and connections to summer programs and opportunities.

INTERNSHIPS AND SUMMER JOBS

Before LBW, I reached out to one of my dad's friends and secured a short internship. Truthfully, internships for high school students are somewhat hard to come by. However, if you are intent on getting an internship, look for something that needs the viewpoint of a high school student. In other words, do a job that's meant for someone your age! A friend of mine wrote for our school's alumni magazine and through those connections found an internship that needed the reflections of a high school student. Also, don't be afraid to start at the bottom. There are plenty of city council offices, museums, colleges, and media outlets that need a gopher, phone answerer, or just someone who helps around the office. Just being in these environments and absorbing what is going on can provide valuable lessons and insights.

Another great way to spend your summer is to do exploration trips or volunteer work. One company, The Road Less Travelled, offers some amazing international philanthropic trips. Alternatively, a lot of my friends have gotten summer jobs. Usually they aren't huge jobs; most involve working at a store or restaurant. But even a minimum-wage, part-time job is a worthwhile way to spend the summer. This demonstrates maturity and responsibility. Colleges love to see students who spent their summer productively, either doing what they love or doing something mature. So however you spend your summer, spend it meaningfully!

FINAL THOUGHTS

- Start early and explore different fields to find your interests.
- Find something that will supplement your education. If you're already planning on taking AP Chemistry, don't take a summer preparatory course just so you'll receive high marks during the school year.
- Get out of the house. Anything is better than sitting around on your computer.

My experience with summer programs has been amazing. I cannot stress enough how important it is to go out and meet bright and motivated individuals. If you aren't sure how to spend your summer, a program is a safe place to start. Of course, setting the summer aside for family, whom you may not see much while you're away at boarding school, is also a worthwhile way of spending a portion of your vacation. Summer is your free time—use it to complement your high school experience and be productive!

ABOUT WENDY HUANG

Originally from Acton, Massachusetts, I attended my town's public schools until the end of ninth grade. In the fall of 2011, I enrolled at boarding school. At St. Paul's School, I am a member of the ballet company and a prefect for my dorm. I also participate in other dance clubs and my school's Gay-Straight Alliance.

CHAPTER 26
Standardized Testing:
A (Stressful) Rite of Passage

by Casey Mulchay
The Thacher School—Ojai, California—Class of 2013
Hometown: Camarillo, California

E very student knows what it's like to take tests. We've all had to do it. I'm sure you know those kids who excel during testing, and you also know people like me, who aren't the best test-takers. Standardized tests are just like any other test, but with the added pressure of a longer testing period and the knowledge that they can be a deciding factor in the boarding school or college admission process. Standardized testing is not something you can really study for; instead, you must prepare and familiarize yourself with the type of test. These tests can be intimidating, but the right preparation can help most students perform better in the testing zone. Let's start by introducing you to the first standardized test you'll probably encounter on your road to and through boarding school.

As part of my application process to The Thacher School, a small boarding school in California's rural Ojai Valley, I had to take a test called the Secondary School Admissions Test (SSAT®). Most independent schools require this test, but you should also check to see if your middle school offers the Independent School Entrance Exam (ISEE), as some boarding schools will allow this test in place of or in addition to the SSAT. The SSAT score is used by the admission department to chart your understanding and potential in verbal, reading, and mathematical subjects and determine if you are capable of holding your own and succeeding at their school. I don't like to prepare for tests, so I've pretty much blocked studying for this test out of my memory! That said, I was already somewhat familiar with the process from taking state-required standardized tests in school, so I felt very comfortable taking it. The test consisted of math, reading, and verbal sections with multiple-choice questions and an essay. The math section isn't too advanced, but it does include some algebra. The reading section has short excerpts to read, and the questions require you to answer analytical questions about their structure and content. The verbal section is filled with analogies and vocabulary questions. Think of this test as your first step into the world of standardized testing throughout your high school career.

Once I was in boarding school, the next test I had to take was the SAT® Reasoning Test (commonly known as just the SAT). This is the test that is probably most familiar (and anxiety-inducing) to students. Most parents and teachers stress over this test because it can impact what might happen to you in the future. There are many theories about how college admission officers look at an application, and many people believe that the first thing reviewed is the test scores. While it's unlikely that a college will base acceptance solely on test scores, standardized tests are still a key factor because they represent the student and his or her promise as a scholar. The SAT evaluates different aspects of the student's knowledge in the same form as the SSAT, with math, reading, essay, and verbal sections, so it's likely that most boarding school students are already somewhat familiar with this type of test. The current SAT is based on 2400 points (800 per section). On the writing portion, two readers evaluate the quality of the essay, and their scores are combined and then factored into the overall score.

NEWS FLASH: *The SAT is changing in 2016! According to the College Board, big changes are coming to this test. For more information about this, see the end of this chapter, and go online to www.collegeboard.org/delivering-opportunity/ sat/redesign.*

I was not very happy with my SAT scores and was advised to take the ACT as well.

The ACT® (American College Test) is similar to SAT, but its format is different and can result in a different level of success for individual students. The ACT sections cover the same subject areas, except for an added science section that includes analyzing graphs and tables and answering multiple-choice questions. The sections in the ACT are also longer. While the SAT has two short sections for each subject, the ACT has one longer section for each subject. Each student can have a different experience with each of these tests, and you may find that one is more comfortable and works better for you. So how do you find out what is the right test for you? And once you do, how do you prepare for it?

My sophomore year, my whole class had to sit for both the PSAT® and the PLAN®, which are shorter previews of the SAT and ACT, respectively, and provide an actual testing environment so students can determine which test better suits them. Since my PSAT and PLAN scores didn't vary much, my college counselors decided that I should take both the SAT and ACT. In addition, I was put into test-prep classes my junior year to prepare me for my standardized tests.

My college counselors also gave me practice versions of the full SAT and ACT to take over the summer before junior year. For these, I sat down and had my mom time me for every section until I completed the entire test. It was almost like the real testing environment, except that it was at my kitchen table instead of a gym full of students. The tests were then sent to a grading company and scored, just like the actual SAT or ACT would be.

In my junior year, I took a college-preparatory class for the first half of the year, but it was primarily a test-prep class. This type of class helped me become familiar with particular types of questions, and it allowed me to take practice tests. If you work well in group settings and can develop your skills from the others around you, I suggest taking a group prep class. But if that just isn't your style, investing in a private tutor can make a huge difference. Basically, the idea is the same: at least twice a week, complete a practice section of the test. You can find practice tests online or in practice books. My class used the *College Board's Official SAT Study Guide*. This book offered multiple tests in addition to sections with helpful hints and answer keys.

After preparation, the next step is actually taking the test. Don't freak out. If you've prepared enough, you are in a great position to take the test. Remember, if you don't do as well as you thought you would, you can take it again. Most people suggest taking your standardized test two or three times. In my case, I took the SAT once, and based on my scores, figured out it was not the right test for me. The college counselors realized that since I was better at math and science (and not so strong in English), the ACT was better for me to take. I took the ACT twice, and ended up sending my second scores to colleges. That's the next good thing—you don't have to send all your scores! But keep in mind that some colleges may require scores from one test and not the other.

Now that I've gone over everything, let's do a little recap. When it comes to standardized testing, the first step is to relax, because the testing process probably won't be as bad as you think it will. Next you need to figure out which test or tests will give you the better result. Do this by taking the PSAT and PLAN. Then prepare for those tests to the best of your ability. Start by taking practice sections of whichever test better suits you. And finally, review your scores after your first test to see if that was really the better choice. It never hurts to take it again or to try a new test.

Here are some helpful hints to think about before and during testing:

- Don't freak out about testing, but also don't blow it off completely. These tests do affect your future, but not too much that you can't recover from your scores.

- Check to see if wrong answers count against you; figure out if guessing can actually help you during a test. This varies among the different tests; for example, the ACT does not penalize you for guessing while the SAT deducts points based on incorrect answers.

- Wear comfortable clothes and shoes, and bring water to the test. I know it may sound silly, but you want to be able to focus on the test, not that your pants are too tight. Also, if you get stuck, sometimes just taking a breath and a sip of water can wake you up a little and help you move past your problem.

- Keep an eye on the clock during the test. Bring a watch to ensure you can check the time if a wall clock isn't easy to see.

- Before you read the passages in the reading comprehension section, read the questions. This helps you know what to look for in the passage.

- Above all, just breathe and prepare, and you will make it through. We might not all be expert test-takers, but we will still survive. Good luck!

ABOUT CASEY MULCHAY

I was first introduced to The Thacher School when my older brother attended and loved it. So when it came time for me to consider high school, I decided to apply. At Thacher, I participated in the horse program, performing arts (theater productions and choir), the dance program, soccer, and the Literary Society. I was also a senior prefect in a junior girls' dorm. I now attend Northeastern University in Boston.

THE REDESIGNED SAT: BIG CHANGES

As noted earlier in this chapter, the SAT is changing in 2016. According to the College Board the redesigned SAT will have these new sections: Evidence-Based Reading and Writing, Math, and the Essay.

The exam will be based on 1600 points—the top scores for the Math section and the Evidence-Based Reading and Writing section will be 800, and the Essay score will be reported separately.

Here are additional key changes for the redesigned SAT, as noted by the College Board:

Relevant Words in Context: Students will need to interpret the meaning of words based on the context of the passage in which they appear. The focus will be on "relevant" words—not obscure ones.

Command of Evidence: In addition to demonstrating writing skills, students will need to show that they're able to interpret, synthesize, and use evidence found in a wide range of sources.

Essay Analyzing a Source: Students will read a passage and explain how the author builds an argument, supporting their claims with actual data from the passage.

Math Focused on Three Key Areas: Problem Solving and Data Analysis (using ratios, percentages, and proportional reasoning to solve problems in science, social science, and career contexts), the Heart of Algebra (mastery of linear equations and systems), and Passport to Advanced Math (more complex equations and the manipulation they require).

Problems Grounded in Real-World Contexts: The questions will be grounded in the real world, directly related to work students will need to perform in college.

Analysis in Science and in Social Studies: Students will need to apply reading, writing, language, and math skills to answer questions in contexts of science, history, and social studies.

Founding Documents and Great Global Conversation: Students will find an excerpt from one of the Founding Documents—such as the Declaration of Independence, the Constitution, and the Bill of Rights—or a text from the "Great Global Conversation" about freedom, justice, and human dignity.

No Penalty for Wrong Answers: Students will earn points for the questions they answer correctly.

If you'll be taking the SAT after March 2016, check out the College Board's website at https://www.collegeboard.org/delivering-opportunity/sat/redesign for the most up-to-date information.

CHAPTER 27
Applying to Colleges: The Next Step

by Vanessa Lizárraga
Cate School—Carpinteria, California—Class of 2012
Hometown: Los Angeles, California

C ollege—the next big step, they say. "It's the best four years of your life," I was told, "so choose wisely." Yes, it's definitely an important choice, and ideally, you and only you should have control of that choice. College signifies real independence, probably even more than boarding school does. College is the first taste you get of true adulthood. College is your initiation into the real world.

I remember being a junior at Cate School, an independent boarding school in Carpinteria, California—knowing absolutely nothing about the college process. Unlike many of my classmates, I didn't have any siblings who had applied to college or parents who attended a U.S. college or university. At that point, I couldn't begin to fathom the complexity of the process, for I was truly a "first-timer."

I was very concerned that my lack of knowledge about the college selection process would put me at a huge disadvantage. I would have to start from the very bottom, by understanding the process well enough to explain it to my parents. I was a first-generation Mexican-American girl from South Central Los Angeles with nothing other than big dreams and the desire to work hard to get a college education and make my family proud. I didn't have the support from home that many of my friends had. Of course, my family wanted me to succeed, but college was simply my responsibility and completely up to me. I couldn't call home and ask my mother to read my essay and give me her opinion, and I couldn't ask my parents to complete my FAFSA application, mainly because they didn't understand what was being asked. I knew I was alone, or at least I thought I was.

These worries came along at the end of my first semester as a junior. And the worries only grew as the pressures of being a senior and taking on more responsibilities loomed closer on the horizon. In mid-January of my junior year, when I thought I was about to drown in a pool of concerns, I received an e-mail from the college counseling office, "All juniors, please meet in the Johnson Library. Your presence is mandatory." I felt the pressure rising. Here comes another list of things to do, I thought.

GETTING STARTED

I showed up at the meeting, along with the other 70 students in my class. Each of us was assigned to one of the school's two full-time college counselors. Now, when I first pictured the relationship I would have with my college counselor, I envisioned the same one I had with my counselor in middle school. Keep in mind I went to a large public school with about 600 kids in my eighth-grade class; therefore, I pictured our relationship would be nonexistent. Happily, that was not at all how it was at Cate.

At Cate, I had an incredible support system, not only from my college counselor, but also from the faculty members on campus. I've always thought of boarding school students as spoiled, and not because of the economic advantages some may have. Unlike many high school students in public high schools around the country, we are surrounded with supportive faculty and classmates. We are given the tools to succeed; then it's up to us to use them for our best interests. We may be in a challenging academic environment with a lot of personal responsibility, but we do have a vast amount of built-in support at our fingertips.

Fortunately, I was assigned a college counselor, Anne Hall, whom I now call my guardian angel. Mrs. Hall not only believed in me from the very beginning, but she pushed me to apply to some of the best institutions in the country by encouraging me to be confident and dream big.

APPLICATIONS, ACCEPTANCES, AND REJECTIONS

By my senior year, I knew I wanted to challenge myself and explore a different kind of environment. Thus, I was set on applying to East Coast schools. My mother, however, was not too happy about this decision, so I decided to apply to a few California schools as well. Soon I had fourteen schools on my list, and I intended to apply to each one. Meeting after meeting, Mrs. Hall reminded me of the time and effort this would take on my part. But I was certain that I wanted to have options, so I kept all fourteen schools on my list.

Out of the fourteen, there was one that meant the most to me, the one school that was always my dream. I decided to apply to Harvard early action. It was the first year the school allowed early action applications, and since it wasn't restrictive, I decided to take a chance and go for it. I put all of my heart, mind, and soul into that application, trying to showcase myself to the best of my abilities. I met with Mrs. Hall a couple of times a week to go over my essays and make sure everything was ready to be submitted. After submitting, I waited and waited, hopeful that the letter or e-mail I would receive would be the best news of my high school career. I got an e-mail the day before Thanksgiving vacation. I had been deferred. It wasn't the end of the world, but I certainly wasn't elated. Like any other senior, I wanted the letter to read "We are happy to offer you admission." I wanted to be jumping for joy, knowing that the next four years of my life were set, just as I had planned.

I was upset and didn't know exactly how to react. The first person I ran to was Mrs. Hall. She was the only person I really trusted on campus when it came to deciding the next four years of my life. She hugged me, and we talked for what seemed like hours. She reminded me that this wasn't a defeat, and that I had better things coming. I tried to put the news behind me and move on. "Life can't stop based on one decision," said Mrs. Hall. I completed all my other applications with no real idea of where I wanted to go. I desperately hoped that one of the other thirteen schools would speak to me. In all honesty, I thought that financial aid might be the deciding factor.

Overall, nothing really went as planned. I remained waitlisted at Harvard, but eleven out of the thirteen others immediately offered me a place at their school. I was able to shorten the list by considering financial aid options, but I still had a choice to make, and I couldn't leave it all up to financial aid. Since I didn't have the means to visit the schools, Mrs. Hall and my advisor helped gather the funds to buy me a plane ticket to visit Brown University and the University of Pennsylvania, the top two schools on my list. After visiting each campus, I had my answer. The school where I knew I had found a home, a place where I could be happy, was Penn. I can't really explain it; I just felt it was the right place for me. I enrolled at Penn, and it has been the best decision I have made in my life thus far.

As boarding school students, we are taught to plan and prepare. But no matter how carefully we plan, things may not always transpire according to those plans. That's life. Things happen for a reason. There's not always a need to question or to be angry when something doesn't go your way. The best we can do is to learn from these experiences and move on. Remember, there's always a plan for us, even if we didn't necessarily plan all the details ourselves.

COLLEGE APPLICATION TIPS

- Plan ahead. Ask your teachers by the end of junior year if they will commit to writing a recommendation. Make sure you let them know far in advance because writing recommendation letters takes quite a bit of time and effort on their part. And be sure to send them a thank-you note once they write the letter.

- Start brainstorming your college essays over the summer. Write a few rough drafts. You may change your mind or decide to write something different once you start applying, but it is definitely good to have thought your essays through early and not have to scramble to think of ideas at the last minute.

- Prepare for your SATs, SAT Subject Tests, and/or ACTs by taking a test-prep course, or by taking as many practice exams as possible. The more you practice, the better you will do when it comes to the real test.

- Not all colleges will require an interview, but you will often have an interview if you apply early to a certain school. The best advice I can give you is to be yourself. Be articulate and clearly get your points across, but always remember to show the interviewer who you are. The interviewer wants to see what sets you apart from the thousands of other applicants. Leave him or her with a good understanding of you as a person and a desire to know more about you.

- Register on the Common Application website at the beginning of the August before your senior year. You should also register at the NCAA Clearinghouse if you want to be considered as a college athlete. Make sure you contact your college counselor if you have any questions about this.

- Write your personal statement on your own. It is an opportunity for you to share a slice of your life with your reader, and it should be in your own voice. Be creative, but don't forget to showcase your best self in writing. For a lot of schools, this is one of the few opportunities they will have to really get to know you, so make it good, eloquent, and, above all, authentic.

- Don't be afraid to brag about yourself (in a controlled manner, of course). Create a student resume listing all of your accomplishments outside of the classroom, (leadership, extracurriculars, awards, honors, athletic participation, summer experiences, jobs, community service, etc.). Everything you have done since the summer after eighth grade counts!

FINAL THOUGHTS

As you approach your senior year and the college selection process, make sure you use your college counselors as resources. They have your best interests at heart and will guide you in the right direction. I recommend that you know what kind of school you are looking for, so you don't end up applying to an insane number of schools (as I did). Plan ahead, but be willing to change your plans along the way. Remember to start working on your essays early. You don't want your schoolwork to interfere with college apps, or vice versa. Also, don't forget to enjoy your senior year. If you're organized and plan accordingly, you'll have time to complete schoolwork and college apps and still enjoy your last year in high school. It will be hard work, but the end result is worth it.

Also, please don't fall into the trap of senioritis! I don't even think it's an actual condition, but rather a concept that seniors devised to justify their lack of energy or desire to work hard. Working hard until the end will make receiving that diploma and all the acceptance letters so much more rewarding. And if you don't get into the school of your dreams, don't be upset. There will be a school out there that will want you and where you will probably be happy. Remember to be confident and strive for only the best. It's your next big step, so make sure it's worth taking. Best of luck!

ABOUT VANESSA LIZÁRRAGA

Attending such a small boarding school gave me the opportunity to truly engage with my classmates and faculty. The Cate community was my family and continues to be, even after graduation. I took advantage of everything Cate had to offer, academically and socially. I was involved in almost every activity on campus as early as my freshman year. I remember the Student Diversity Leadership/People of Color Conference the most. I had an incredible time in New Orleans, and it was the first time I had the opportunity to represent Cate away from the campus. In my sophomore year, I started the multicultural club on campus, stressing Latino culture. This club educated our community about our culture and showcased diversity. I also joined the Cate newspaper staff, starting as a writer and later becoming head of the sports section. I was one of two Head Senior Prefects on campus my senior year. Now I am at the University of Pennsylvania, majoring in biology with a premed concentration and a minor in Japanese. I can't wait for what academic, extracurricular, and social adventures will come my way in the future!

Concluding Remarks

I hope that you have found *The Boarding School Survival Guide* to be a helpful resource that has given you additional ideas and insights into the boarding school process. I think the diverse collection of honest opinions and voices within this book really captures the essence of the boarding school experience.

Boarding school thus far has been a fantastic chapter of my life, and this book is really meant to help you figure out if it's the right choice for you, too.

Best of luck on your boarding school journey!

~ Justin Ross Muchnick

Useful Resources for Boarding School Students

The list below is a collection of resources shared, recommended, and suggested by the contributors to *The Boarding School Survival Guide*. As you know, this book was written to give of information that I felt was missing or hard to access in my boarding school research process, namely the voices and ideas shared by actual current students and graduates of boarding schools. The sites and resources below also assisted me and many of my contributors in our process of researching, applying, and living the boarding school experience. I hope they will help you, too!

HELPFUL WEBSITES AND ONLINE RESOURCES TO RESEARCH BOARDING SCHOOLS

School websites: Visit each of these to find information on faculty, campus activities and traditions, course guides, and most everything else you need to know about the specifics of each particular school.

School newspapers: Read what students have to say today about their school right now. Many student newspapers are uncensored by the school (inquire if you are curious), so students' real voices and opinions can be heard. Most school papers can be found online, but you can also e-mail the school to request that a few issues be mailed to you.

Facebook pages, Twitter feeds, Instagram: All easy, quick places to collect information, get current news, and ask questions of the schools you are interested in.

boardingschools.com: A helpful resource for students and families researching schools. Offers behind-the-scenes looks at over 300 schools across the United States, Canada, and abroad. Also known as The Association of Boarding Schools (TABS). Check them out on Facebook, too.

boardersreport.com: This website covers news from boarding schools around the world.

boardspacemag.com: Boardspace Magazine is an international online magazine with content provided by current boarding school students and recent graduates on a wide range of topics. Here is some information from the "About" section of this very cool site. Be sure to check it out:

"Boardspace is an international online hub for anyone connected to a boarding school. This is a chance to compare notes with people out of your school's 'bubble.' At Phillips Exeter Academy (and a few other schools), there's a teaching method called Harkness. The Harkness method is a teaching style in which a group of students sit around an oval table with their teacher, and instead of raising hands in the class, they have a conversation. Everyone brings something to the table, and every voice is equal. We want yours. Think of us as an online Harkness table where the conversation never stops. Have a seat. Welcome to Boardspace."

boardingschoolreview.com: A useful place to start to research and compare schools and to determine what you might want in your boarding school experience. The content is mostly data-driven, but there are some articles, too.

CollegeConfidential.com: A community bulletin board/forum with an area dedicated to prep school students and parents. You will need to dig through a fair amount of message boards to find boarding school information, but it is there.

theexeterdresscode.tumblr.com: Another fun online community and student-run blog that gives you the feel of boarding school life, with a look at on-campus fashion and how it is interpreted at a boarding school with a dress code. Taft and Hotchkiss also have "Lookbooks" that you might want to check out if boarding school attire is your thing.

adventuresinboardingschool.tumblr.com: A question-and-answer site and space to seek and share boarding school information.

ACADEMIC AND BOARDING SCHOOL SUPPORT RESOURCES FOR STUDENTS

Blackboard Collaborate: A cool, collaborative site where students can obtain support from other students, teachers, and educators on a variety of subjects.

Evernote: A cloud-based note-taking service that "can sync text-based notes and other media across desktop and mobile devices."

home.brainfuse.com: An amazing website that offers online tutoring, which can assist in tough courses like calculus. It's really cool—there are teachers who provide homework help in an instant-message format.

ibscrewed.livejournal.com/profile: A student message and discussion board and resource location for students participating in the International Baccalaureate (IB) program and other competitive academic endeavors.

Infogr.am: Helpful site to produce and create illustrations for data in research papers or presentations.

OmmWriter (www.ommwriter.com): This is an audio-visual writing app that offers different music and writing backgrounds.

owl.english.purdue.edu/: A helpful site to use when writing papers to determine proper MLA format.

Prezi.com: A great site to assist with creation, collaboration, and presentation of school work or projects.

RescueTime.com: This website helps track the time you spend on certain activities, and it can block distracting websites for the hours you set, so you can focus better and be more productive.

StudyBlue: A flashcard site where you can make and share your study aids.

Quizlet: This is a site to create flashcard sets and other study tools.

WhiteRoom: This app helps Mac users write without distractions. Requires Mac OS X 10.7+.

FINANCIAL AID RESOURCES

Admissions Quest (www.admissionsquest.com/~financialaid/index.cfm/articletypeid/7): Articles and links about ways to afford boarding school.

Be A Prep Kid (http://beaprepkid.com): Nonprofit and independent organization founded in 2008 that helps youth attend different types of prep schools.

FinAid for Private Schools (www.privateschools.com/financialaid.phtml): Detailed information about paying for private schools.

Jack Kent Cooke Foundation (www.jkcf.org/): A private, independent foundation, established in 2000 by Jack Kent Cooke, to advance the education of exceptionally promising students who have financial need.

Scholarships.com (https://www.scholarships.com/financial-aid/college-scholarships/scholarships-by-grade-level/high-school-scholarships/): While this site is primarily geared toward college scholarships, it can also be used to search for high school scholarships.

Search Engines: Try typing "scholarships for high school" or a similar phrase into various search engines, such as About.com, Google, Bing, etc. to look for additional listings and possibilities.

Resources used for Chapter 3, Financial Aid: Paying for Boarding School

- http://www.yorkavenuepreschool.org/pdf/Six Steps to Understanding Financial Aid.pdf
- http://www.act.org/path/parent/finaid/questions.html
- http://www.privateschools.com/financialaid.phtml
- http://exeter.edu/admissions/109_1371.aspx
- http://exeter.edu/admissions/109_7844.aspx
- http://www.newhampton.org/financialaid
- http://www.lacademy.edu/page.cfm?p=365
- http://www.admissionsquest.com

Other Books about Boarding Schools

No, this book isn't the last word on boarding schools. They're hard to find, but they are out there. Here are some nonfiction books and novels that might offer you additional information and insights into the boarding school experience.

After the Harkness Gift: A History of Phillips Exeter Academy Since 1930, Julia Heskel and David Dyer (Exeter, N.H.: Phillips Exeter Academy, 2008). The origins and impact of this unique independent learning style.

The Best of the Best: Becoming Elite at an American Boarding School, Ruben A. Gaztimbide-Fernandez (Cambridge, Mass.: Harvard University Press, 2009). A peek into a U.S. boarding school from an author who spent two years on the inside researching it.

Prep, Curtis Sittenfeld (New York: Random House, 2005). Novel about a girl and her boarding school drama.

Private Secondary Schools 2014–15, 35th edition (Albany, N.Y.: Peterson's, 2013). A comprehensive reference and information guide to boarding schools as well as private day, military, and special-needs schools.

The Starboard Sea, Amber Dermont (London: Corsair, 2013). Novel about student experiences, drama, and social issues set in a New England boarding school.

The Boarding School Survival Guide
Scholarship Contest

Two lucky and worthy readers of *The Boarding School Survival Guide* will receive $1,000 each toward their boarding school tuition scholarship. The author, Justin Muchnick, is awarding the two scholarships to current or future boarding school students. The award winners will be determined at the sole discretion of the author, Justin Muchnick.

Peterson's Nelnet, LLC, and its respective affiliates and trademark licenses, is not a sponsor of this scholarship award.

SCHOLARSHIP CONTEST SUBMISSION GUIDELINES

ESSAY PROMPT: Please write an essay of about 500 words, offering your thoughts on why you want to attend boarding school—your reasons, desires, discoveries, and so on. Also, please address why this scholarship will be helpful to you in your boarding school process and journey or why you feel that you are a worthwhile recipient. Feel free to share personal anecdotes, too.

Please e-mail your submission with the subject heading "Scholarship" to Justin Muchnick at: boardingschoolsurvival@gmail.com

Deadline: June 30, 2015. Winners will be announced and contacted during the summer of 2015 to receive their scholarship award. The scholarship will be paid directly to your boarding school (or future boarding school) to be earmarked to defray the cost of tuition. All submissions become the property of Justin Muchnick, and any portion of your submission may be published in the future in a book by Justin Muchnick or in any media outlet when announcing the prize winners.

Please see next page and include the following language with your submission and signature via scan or PDF in an e-mail, or the form will be sent to you via e-mail upon receipt of your submission and will require your completion before your submission is reviewed.

The Boarding School Survival Guide Scholarship Consent Form

I, (name) _____ , consent to have my submission (possibly) published in media outlets or a future edition of this book or other publication if selected as a winner. I certify by my signature below that my submission is my own work and does not violate any copyright laws or other proprietary rights of third parties.

Date: _____

Print Full Name: _____

Signature: _____

Date of Birth: _____

Current School: _____

Home Mailing Address: _____

_____

City, State: _____

ZIP Code: _____

E-mail Address: _____

Expected Boarding School Graduation Date: _____